THE LION IN LOVE

Also by Shelagh Delaney:

A TASTE OF HONEY (E-159)

THE
LION IN LOVE

A PLAY BY
Shelagh Delaney

GROVE PRESS, INC.   NEW YORK

This play was first presented by Wolf Mankowitz at the Belgrade Theatre, Coventry, on 5 September 1960.

On 29 December 1960 the play was presented by the English Stage Company in association with Wolf Mankowitz at the Royal Court Theatre, London, with the following cast:

ANDY	John Rees
JESSE	Howard Goorney
PEG	Patricia Healey
BANNER	Kenneth Cope
FRANK	Garfield Morgan
CROSS-LANE NORA	Diana Coupland
KIT	Patricia Burke
LOLL	Peter Fraser
NELL	Renny Lister
ENA	Margery Mason
LENA	Jeanette Hider
LOCAL TOWNSPEOPLE	Juliet Alliston, Anthony Beeston, Brian Croft, Maureen Dormer, Dermot McDowell
GUITARISTS	Martin Kershaw and John Bennett

Directed by CLIVE BARKER
Designed by UNA COLLINS

The play is set in a town in the North of England

ACT I Saturday. St. Valentine's Day
ACT II Saturday. Some weeks later
ACT III Sunday. The following week

The Lion by chance saw a fair maid, the Forester's Daughter, as she was tripping over a lawn, and fell in love with her. Nay, so violent was his passion that he could not live unless he made her his own; so that, without any more delay, he spoke his mind to the father and demanded the damsel for his wife. The man, odd as the proposal seemed at first, yet soon recollected that, complying, he might get the Lion into his power, but that by refusing he should only exasperate and provoke his rage. He therefore consented, but told him it must be upon these conditions: that, considering the girl was young and tender he must agree to let his teeth be plucked out, and his claws cut off, lest he should hurt her, or at least frighten her with the apprehension of them. The Lion was too much in love to hesitate; but was no sooner deprived of his teeth and claws than the treacherous Forester attacked him with a huge club and knocked his brains out.

MORAL

Nothing can be more fatal to peace than the ill-assorted marriages into which rash love may lead.

Aesop—Fable CIX

Act One

The time is the present. Saturday afternoon.

The scene is a city in northern England. A section of the street and a house. Only the lower room is visible and the house is suggested rather than real. Across the back wall of the room is a flight of stairs. Behind the stairs the city can be seen surrounding the house like a fantastic panorama. The street area contains a lamp-post and a road block and behind this the local bombed-site can be seen.

ANDY *is slowly performing a few simple acrobatics on the road-block while* JESSE *sits reading a newspaper.*

The quiet rhythm of this is broken by the appearance of PEG *and* MAUREEN *who run on from the market playing tag.*

MAUREEN *knocks* ANDY *off his bars. He chases her off.*

MAUREEN: Alley oop!
ANDY: Oh, knock it off will you. . . .
MAUREEN: Ta'ra, Peg.
PEG: See you!
JESSE: Leave the lad alone, he was doing very nicely there!

[ANDY *returns.*]

ANDY: She could've killed me.
PEG: That would've saved me the trouble. You look like a monkey swinging around on them bars.

ANDY: I've got to practise.

PEG: What for?

ANDY: I might start working in the circuses again.

PEG: Oh, yes, and pigs might fly too. I wish I could afford to stay at home all day doing nothing. It must be nice.

JESSE: I've done my share of work.

PEG: That lazy devil hasn't. [*Pause.*] Oh! I'm fagged out.

JESSE: Fagged out! My God! You've no stamina whatsoever, girl. A good day's work puts you flat on your back. I'm not telling a word of a lie—when I was half your age I worked seven days a week, all the hours God sent, and for a fraction of the money young people get paid these days. I've heaved coal in Pendlebury Pit, I've dug holes in the road with buck niggers. I've worked harder in one day than you'll ever work in a fortnight.

ANDY: I've never known you fond of hard work, old man.

PEG: Anyway, times have changed. Everything's provided for us now. We can afford to lounge around here in the lush playgrounds of the world.

JESSE: Business any good on the market today?

PEG: Fair to middling. There wasn't much money about though.

JESSE: I didn't think there would be. I didn't see many people pass this way.

PEG: There was only a handful of 'em. I don't know where they all get to. Seems to be less people around every week.

JESSE: I can remember the Saturday afternoons when I couldn't sit here reading my paper for the crowds passing by on the way to the market. Hundreds of 'em. Used to be like a circus. You'd have thought they were hanging some poor devil in the Town Hall Square. Many a time I've narrowly escaped being trampled to death in the rush.

PEG: The market was dead by three o'clock this afternoon.

JESSE: Everything seems dead lately round here. How many people have walked past us this afternoon, Andy?

ANDY: Half a dozen. . . .

JESSE: And d'you know why? Supermarkets. People are getting lazy. They won't buy anything now unless it's been picked, plucked and packed away in a polythene bag. That Supermarket down the road puts the fear of God into me. I went in there once—never again—I was herded and hounded through little barbed wire fences till I didn't know whether I was buying or being sold.

ANDY: Did your dad take much money this afternoon, Kiddo?

PEG: You mind your own business and I'll mind mine.

ANDY: Come on, tell us how much you're worth, Peg. If you've got enough, I might marry you.

PEG: Huh! If all the men in the world looked like you I'd stick to women.

JESSE: She's worth a small fortune on the side, this girl, you know. . . .

PEG: Oh yes. I'll get rich working for my father, right enough.

JESSE: You only work for him on Saturdays—you don't do that for money—you do it for love.

PEG: He gives me sixpence for every quid he earns—and you know how much he makes, don't you . . . I make more than that at the office during the week.

JESSE: Do you want to earn yourself some ready cash now then by doing your old grandfather a favour?

PEG: What is it and how much do I get for doing it?

JESSE: I backed a couple of winners this afternoon. Go and collect my winnings from the bookies—

PEG: You're always gambling.

JESSE: I'll give you ten per cent. How's that?

PEG: Generous.

JESSE: I'm a generous feller.

PEG: Just let me rest for a bit then.

JESSE: If you rest much more, you'll lose the use of your legs.
   [*Pause.*]

PEG: Where's my mother?

JESSE: She hasn't come back yet.

ANDY: She's still down at the station—the police are keeping her for a mascot.

PEG: You shut up and don't be so cheeky.

ANDY: Don't tell me to shut up, I was the only one who went down to the court to see her charged. None of her own family bothered.

JESSE: Aye, well we can't stand the shame of it. She's a bit of a problem is your mother.

PEG: We know—she takes after her dad.

JESSE: She broke my record for drunk and disorderly a long while ago.

PEG: What happened to her this time then?

ANDY: Fined two pound and bound over to keep the peace.

JESSE. It's all here in the evening paper. [*He reads.*] Market Trader's Wife Bound Over. This morning Mrs. Kathleen Fresko, unemployed, of 25 Lichfield Street, The Market Place, appeared before a special court charged with being drunk and disorderly and with resisting arrest. The Court was told of her twenty-seven previous convictions mainly for being drunk and disorderly, insulting behaviour, assault and once attempting suicide. The magistrate fined her two pounds for being drunk and disorderly and on the other charge bound her over for two years to keep the peace. On leaving the court Mrs. Fresko thanked the magistrate and said: "I was brought here in a taxi. Can I have a taxi home?"

ANDY: Bloody cheek.

PEG: But that was early this morning, she should be home by now.

JESSE: She'll be back at the police station. She forgets sometimes that she doesn't actually live there.

ANDY: It's nice and warm at the station. She's probably having a cup of tea there while she's waiting for the pubs to open.

PEG: Will you keep your mouth shut please and don't talk about my mother like that.

JESSE: Your mother'll come back home when she's good and ready, Peg. Don't worry about her—

PEG: Well, you know what she's like. If she's not careful she'll finish up one night in some back alley with a knife stuck in her back.

JESSE: We've all got to go sometime and that way's as good as any. Your mother's like an animal, girl, and she'd prefer to die outside under a bush rather than pop off in a nice clean bed in the front parlour. Now stop hanging about. Go and do my errand or the bookies'll be shut.

PEG: You never give me a minute's peace, do you. Are you coming with me, Andy?

ANDY: No, I'll hang on here.

PEG: O.K. Suit yourself.

[*She rushes away. As she moves off her elder brother* BANNER *enters, carrying a suitcase.*]

BANNER: Hallo, Grandad!

JESSE: Well, look who's here? Banner! I never expected to see you again.

BANNER: How are you, Grandad?

JESSE: Well, I don't want to sound boasting or conceited, but I'm a bloody fine feller for me age. How's yourself, son?

BANNER: I've never felt better and I've never looked better. And how's my little sister?

PEG: All right. How long have you come home for and when can we look forward to your going back?

BANNER: I knew you'd be pleased to see me—Andy. [*He salutes* ANDY.]

ANDY: Banner.

JESSE: You're as welcome as three fiddlers in May.

ANDY: Looking very prosperous too.

JESSE: What're you doing with yourself these days, young feller-me-lad?

BANNER: Oh! . . . This and that.

ANDY: Makes no odds what he's doing so long as it pays well.

BANNER: It pays all right.

JESSE: Don't spend your money all at once.

JANNER: I don't.

BESSE: But on the other hand remember there aren't any pockets in a shroud.

BANNER [*handing the old man a parcel*]: Present for you.

JESSE: Let's have a look at it. I don't care what it is so long as I can drink it. By God!

ANDY: You can drink that all right.

JESSE: Best brandy.

ANDY: Cigars too.

JESSE: I'll save these for Christmas.

PEG: Christmas is a long way off.

JESSE: You couldn't have done better, Banner. Thanks very much.

BANNER: There's yours, Peg. [*He hands her a parcel. It is a music box.*] It's a good 'un. The best for the best.

[*She fumbles with it, raises the lid, listens as it plays, then snaps the lid down.*]

PEG: Thanks, Banner.

BANNER: D'you like it?

PEG: 'Course I do.

BANNER: Are you sure. You're not just. . . .

PEG: No, I like it.

BANNER: If you don't want it just say so and I'll give you the money instead.

PEG: Oh! For goodness sake! I like it. What else do you want me to do. Have a fit?

BANNER: She's come on a bit since I last saw her.

ANDY: Yes—the sex kitten of the city now.

PEG: Don't be so cheeky, you.

BANNER: Where is everybody?

PEG: Working. Where do you expect?

BANNER: Dad still on the markets ?

JESSE: He'll never be anywhere else.

BANNER: Has he got his own stall yet ?

JESSE: No—he's still selling out of the old suitcase. He's changed his line though. He's selling atom bombs and death ray guns and shrunken heads now—you know— novelties for the kiddies.

BANNER: What about my mam ? Is she still working ?

JESSE: Only when she can't avoid it.

BANNER: I'm dying to see her—and me Dad too. Haven't seen 'em for ages.

JESSE: Not since you got demobbed.

PEG: Why haven't you been home since then ?

ANDY: He's a man of importance now, can't you see that ? Look at the style of him.

PEG: He could still come home for a few days now and again. Still it's nice of you to spare your poor relations a few hours of your time.

BANNER: Don't be so bad tempered.

PEG: Well, it's true.

JESSE: Stop fighting with him.

PEG: Shut up.

BANNER: Don't speak to the old man like that.

PEG: I'm sorry.

JESSE: It's all right. Peg and myself came to an understanding a long time ago. It's the duty of one generation to fight the next.

BANNER: She's horrible.

ANDY: We know, but she's fair about it. She's horrible to everybody.

BANNER: Courting yet ?

PEG: 'Course I am. Men follow me about like little dogs.

ANDY: Ah! Well, we know what that makes her, don't we ?

PEG: Don't be so rude.

BANNER: You courting yet, Andy ?

ANDY: Too expensive.

BANNER: Team up with Peg—she looks the cheap type.

ANDY: I've no romantic interests in Peggy. We're just good friends.

JESSE: Good friends! My God! I'll tell you something, young feller, any man worth his salt coming face to face with this girl ought to give full rein to his God-given instincts.

PEG: Kind of you to say so.

JESSE: My pleasure.

PEG: Mind you, at your age your mind shouldn't be on women.

JESSE: There's still a spark in this old plug. Now then, what's happening to you young men. Are you hungry? Come on, Peg, get in the house and cook these lads a meal.

BANNER: Yes, I'll start off with clear soup, then fish, salmon I think, smoked. Then a portion of meat, fillet steak medium done, with green vegetables, potatoes and gravy. Then we'll have fresh fruit and cream.

ANDY: And we'll finish up with coffee and cigars in the lounge.

PEG: You'll have fish and chips and like it. Come out with me tonight, Banner. To a dance?

BANNER: No.

PEG: Go on. It's a Saint Valentine's night dance. A lot of your old friends'll be there. Come on.

BANNER: I don't like dancing.

PEG: You used to.

BANNER [indicating ANDY]: He'll take you—dancing's more in his line.

PEG: I'm not interested in him. You can come—what's up with you?

BANNER: Oh, knock it off, will you.

PEG: Lend me some money then.

BANNER: I haven't been home five minutes and she's cadging already.

PEG: Just a few shillings.

BANNER: Are you so hard up?

PEG: I'm always hard up.

ANDY: We've been thinking of sending her out to find part time work in one of them little brothels down in Trafford Road.

BANNER: They'd have her on piece work in next to no time.

[FRANK *enters, carrying his suitcase home from the market.*]

PEG: Hey, Dad, look who's come to see you.

FRANK: Well, what blew you in?

BANNER: How's life, Dad?

FRANK: Not too bad, perked up a bit with seeing you. You're looking fit. Still giving them the old one-two, eh? What are you doing up here—fighting at Belle Vue or something?

BANNER: No. I gave up the boxing game. Jacked it in. No future in it.

FRANK: Why?

BANNER: Well, they don't go for boxers these days. All they want is sloggers.

FRANK: There's always room for a good boxer.

BANNER: Well, I gave it up. I thought it was time I went for something bigger. Something with a bit more future in it.

FRANK: Well, you ought to find this lazy devil something to do while you're at it. I'm sick of seeing him loll around.

[*He indicates* ANDY.]

JESSE: He needs shoving back in the zoo.

FRANK: He needs something. I'll bet there are any number of circuses'd sign him up like a shot.

BANNER: Still doing the old physical jerks?

ANDY: Fit as a fiddle.

FRANK: You ought to get cracking properly then, instead of hanging about. Before you know where you are you'll be too old to be turning cartwheels.

ANDY: I'd be turning cartwheels now if it hadn't been for my sister.

FRANK: Is she the only woman you can work with?

ANDY: Well, we'd done the act together since we were kids. You can't just start all over again with somebody else. She was a silly devil. Fancy getting married! Just like a stupid woman.

FRANK: She's probably happier married.

ANDY: Not with the sour-faced bleeder she got chained up to. They've got a baby now. Just like its father—dead ugly. Anyway, what's all this worrying about me for? I'm all right. Never catch me short of money.

JESSE: It's not the money we're worried about so much as how you get hold of it. We're worried about your soul.

ANDY: You worry about my soul then—I'll worry about my pocket.

FRANK: He's up to something and I'll lay ten to one it's something he's not proud of.

ANDY: Do I look like a villain?

JESSE: If you looked like a villain there'd be nothing to worry about. It's the angel faces who cause all the trouble. Still, if he's happy.

BANNER: I hope you don't mind me coming home so unexpectedly.

FRANK: You can come whenever you feel like it. Take this upstairs, love, will you?

PEG: Right. Shall I take yours in too?

BANNER: Thanks.

[PEG *takes the cases into the house.*]

FRANK: How long are you home for?

BANNER: Oh, till I feel like going.

FRANK: Sounds all right, doesn't it?

ANDY: Must be a good job he's got.

FRANK: Yes. What is this job?

BANNER: You've no need to worry. I've got plans.

FRANK: Plans for what?

BANNER: For what I'm going to do.

FRANK: Well, what are you going to do?

BANNER: It's just one of those things Dad, it's all a bit up in the air at the moment but give me time, six months and I'll be well away. You know how it is—I've got to sign things and get it all worked out for certain.

FRANK: What sort of deal is it?

BANNER: You've no need to worry about me. I've got plenty of money and I'm doing very nicely. Well I mean, you've got to plan for your future.

ANDY: Sounds nice.

FRANK: Sounds bloody marvellous.

[KIT *and* NORA *enter from the market, pushing Nora's cart.* KIT *is fooling about and does not notice* BANNER.]

Here's your mother.

JESSE: The white man's burden.

FRANK: Where've you been, Kit?

KIT: You don't ask me where I've been and I won't tell you where to go.

BANNER: Hello, Mam.

KIT: When did you turn up?

BANNER: Not so long ago.

KIT: Thought you'd forgotten where you lived.

BANNER: I've been busy. You know how it is.

KIT: No, I don't know how it is. You can write, can't you?

JESSE: He doesn't write because he knows you can't read.

KIT: Is it worth it, I often wonder. You suffer bringing kids into the world, you wear yourself out keeping one end full and the other end dry, and as soon as they're able they're off and away. Out of sight, out of mind.

NORA: Well, he's back now, so why worry?

[FRANK *enters the house.*]

Hello, love.

BANNER: Hello, Nora.

NORA: It's nice to see you.

BANNER: It's nice to see you. How's the clothes business?

NORA: It's a living. Staying home long?

BANNER: Maybe.

NORA: I hope so. We hardly see anything of you.

BANNER: Well, you know how it is.

NORA: You're looking well, anyway.

KIT: Come over here, Banner. You've been away so long I've almost forgotten what you look like. Put on weight, haven't you? Getting fat. Soft living. Shoulders on him like a ton of bricks.

BANNER: Yes. . . .

KIT: Nice suit you're wearing. Paid for it yet?

BANNER: Paid cash on the nail.

KIT: Good. I'm all right for a couple of bob then. I know where to come when I'm on the tap. It's nice to be able to pay cash for things instead of spending half your life trying to get out of debt.

FRANK [inside the house]: There's only one person in this house gets into debt. And I'm the one who falls for paying them off.

KIT: Well, you're the man of the house. You're responsible for my actions. That's why you married me. To love and cherish. Aw, come on loverlips, smile.

NORA: I'll be going now. I'll see you all later. Give us a lift with the cart, will you Jesse?

JESSE: I'll give you a lift anytime. . . .

NORA: I said the cart.

[He pinches her.]

Oh! you dirty old man.

[BANNER and ANDY act as starters in a race. They move the road block. BANNER holds his hand up, whistles and NORA and JESSE push the cart off.]

ANDY: Watch that old man, Nora.

NORA: I can deal with him, don't you worry.

BANNER: Be careful. He's old enough to know what he wants to do.

KIT [*shouting after them*]: Yes, but is he young enough to do it?

[*She enters the house.*]

KIT: Oh—I must have a sit down.

FRANK: It's a wonder your backside isn't the size of a ten-ton truck—you spend so much time sitting on it. How did you go on in court this morning?

KIT: Oh, they bound me over for two years to keep the peace and fined me a couple of quid.

FRANK: And who's going to pay that?

KIT: Don't get worked up about it, it's already been paid.

FRANK: Who on . . .

KIT: Never you mind. I've got friends.

FRANK: It's a bloody good job too because I couldn't have paid it. What would you do if nobody had paid it?

KIT: They'd probably have put me in prison.

FRANK: That might have been a good thing too for everybody concerned. If you spent a couple of years behind bars you'd appreciate what you've got here a bit more than you do.

KIT: Frank, I wasn't drunk last night. All I was doing was singing a little song. . . .

FRANK: I know what your little songs are like. . . .

KIT: And doing a little dance. What harm is there in that? There was about forty people watching me performing and they were enjoying it too but they hadn't got the bloody courage to get up and dance with me. They hadn't got the courage. Everybody's scared to death of getting into trouble with the police and if it isn't the police they're scared of, then it's the neighbours and if it isn't the bloody neighbours it's the relations. I don't know what's happening to people. They seem scared of their own shadows at times. But the police know my face. That's why I always get caught. Victimization—that's what it is—and another little stripe on some cockeyed constable's navy blue suit. What harm is there in a song and dance?

FRANK: If there's anything worse than the sight of a drunken man, it's the sight of a drunken woman.

KIT: A woman's got as much right—and more cause—to get as drunk as any man.

FRANK: Understand this much. If you get into trouble once more, just once more, don't expect any help from me because you won't get it—I've had enough—don't expect me to pay any more fines or debts because I won't—I'm sick of it.

KIT: You're my husband.

FRANK: I don't care what I am. It's getting beyond a joke. I think you're dollalleytap or something—

KIT: Oh! I must take my shoes off. Huh! Hell hath no fury like a woman's corns, has it?

FRANK: I suppose you've been drinking this afternoon, haven't you?

KIT: I haven't got any money.

FRANK: You've got friends.

KIT: I know—they lead me astray.

FRANK: When are you going to start acting your age?

KIT: When Nelson gets his eye back.

FRANK: I don't suppose you remembered to go and see about that job you were offered, did you?

KIT: I did. That surprised you, didn't it?

FRANK: How did you go on then?

KIT: No luck. It wasn't my fault either. I was more than willing to join the firm. I had a very pleasant interview with the works manager. He told me all about the job and what I'd get paid for doing it. It sounded all right so I said I'd take it; then do you know what he turned round and said? I'm sorry, madam, but if you're prepared to do all the work we demand for the wages we pay then I'm afraid you're not intelligent enough to be employed by us. And so saying he showed me what the door was for.

FRANK: What a tale our cat's got.

KIT: It's the truth.

FRANK: You wouldn't recognize the truth if I gave it to you on a plate for a birthday present.

KIT: Work's hard to find.

FRANK: Anything's hard to find if you go around looking for it with your eyes shut. It's about time you pulled yourself together and realized that you're not a kid any more.

KIT: I'm an old woman—

FRANK: You look like an old woman sometimes. You give as much attention to yourself as you do to this house—

KIT: Oh, are we back to the house again—

FRANK: You ought to look after it—

KIT: Why? That's the hole in the ceiling where the rats fell through last Christmas, isn't it—it's no use standing on the chairs, madam, the bugs round here can jump ten feet—

FRANK: You care for nothing.

KIT: It's clean.

FRANK: Yes, but no thanks to you.

KIT: Peg looks after it very well. Give the girl a medal.

FRANK: Peg's been cleaning this house since she was a kid. No girl enjoys housework—not before they're married anyway.. They want a bit of fun.

KIT: She has enough fun. Here—have a cigarette. Been warm this afternoon, hasn't it. Lovely day for quarrelling.

FRANK: You should look after this house. Peg's out at work all day, apart from anything else.

KIT: Oh! Frank, knock it off. Stop nagging for goodness sake. I'm not up to it. I'm liable to flake out at any minute.

FRANK: You'd be doing me a favour if you flaked out for good.

KIT: Now we're getting at the truth of it. What a thing to say. What a thing to wish your wife dead.

FRANK: Don't talk daft.

KIT: I should've ended it before now.

FRANK: Don't joke about it.

KIT: And I'll try again if you're not careful. You wouldn't stop me, though, would you? You'd watch me die, and be glad about it. Don't try and pretend any different. I can see it in your face. You're bad, you are. Pity for none and especially for me—if you knew how I feel sometimes—[*She starts to play-act.*]—you couldn't know though—it's beyond your mental powers. Everybody thinks I enjoy getting drunk but do you know why I drink—?

FRANK: No. I don't. Why?

KIT: —to forget—half a dozen glasses of whisky take the edge off life—everybody thinks I'm the glad girl of the saloon bar—good for a song and a bit of a dance but it's not so. Pagliacci—that's me.

FRANK: Oh! My palpitations!

KIT: You can laugh but I could swear my heart's breaking inside me sometimes—I can feel it cracking—like now—just put your hand there. Can't you feel it? Oh, Frank, if this isn't the finish of it all I don't know what it is. [PEG *comes downstairs.*] Peggy, come here, love, and let me look at you—it might be the last time. . . .

PEG: Oh! Is she dying again? Shall I wash her down now? It'll save time tomorrow.

FRANK: You go through her pockets, Peg, and see if there's anything worth having there and I'll nip upstairs and dust the death policies. . . .

KIT: That's it—that's right—rattle her bones over the stones, she's only a beggar whom nobody owns. . . .

PEG: Come on, isn't it time we were going to the party?

KIT: Oh God, I'd forgotten all about that.

PEG: Well, hurry up, we'll be late.

FRANK: You're not coming for a start.

[*Exit* FRANK *to kitchen.*]

PEG: Why not?

FRANK [*off*]: For one thing you weren't invited.

PEG: I don't have to be invited to this party—it's only their wedding anniversary.

KIT: Wedding anniversary? Makes you wonder, doesn't it? Some people get married and twenty years after they still feel like celebrating. Makes you wonder where they keep their brains.

FRANK [*off*]: Some people walk on them.

KIT: Aye, but most people sit on them. Well, Peg, your father's spoken. No party for you tonight. It's all for the best really —it's likely to turn a bit wild towards the end and you're too young for that sort of thing.

PEG: Makes me sick.

FRANK [*off*]: Then be sick.

PEG: I bet it's a rotten party anyway. You'll only get drunk.

KIT: I'll bring you back a bottle of lemonade.

[KIT *goes upstairs. Outside the house,* BANNER *and* ANDY.]

BANNER: Whenever I come home me mother and father always seem to be shouting at each other.

ANDY: That's happy married life for you.

BANNER: You can keep it as far as I'm concerned.

ANDY: Fancy a drink down at the pub?

BANNER: May as well—smoke?

ANDY: Ta. Nice case—gold?

BANNER: Good investment. I always buy the best. Never know when you'll have to do a bit of pawning. Lovely job this—cost a packet too.

ANDY: Looks like it. You certainly made your bomb before you quit boxing.

BANNER: The money was good while it lasted but I got fed up with it—scared of finishing up punchy, I suppose.

ANDY: You had a good run though while it lasted. Nearly made the big time.

BANNER: Aye, nearly.

ANDY: Got a couple of battle scars there—

BANNER: Yes—the girls don't half go for 'em too.

ANDY: What are you going to do then?

BANNER: Well, I've been thinking of travelling. I saw quite a bit of the world when I was in the army.

ANDY: So?

BANNER: I want to see more.

ANDY: I've seen it, mate, and believe me one part of the world is as bad as another.

BANNER: That's your opinion. I'm a new boy.

ANDY: You know what I'd do if I were you? I'd find myself a nice girl, get a nice little house somewhere and a couple of babies and settle down.

BANNER: You practice what you preach.

ANDY: I will do when I find the right girl—trouble is I'm too choosey.

BANNER: I'm thinking of getting out of this country. There's nothing much happening over here. I want to go where I can be somebody instead of just being anybody. I'll try one of these new countries, I think.

ANDY: Yes, out in the bush, in the wild, unexplored territory with the natives all running round wild and naked—that's old stuff, boy. The world isn't like that any more. You're still at the cowboys and Indians stage.

BANNER: So what?

ANDY: It's a nice stage to be at, nothing wrong with it at all—poor boy—mental age two and a half but he's very sweet.

BANNER: I'll clobber you in a minute.

ANDY: You couldn't catch me—

BANNER: Come here. Seriously. Why don't you come out there with me. We could go all the way round the world.

ANDY: Not likely. I'm staying put for the time being. I want money in my pocket before I start floating.

BANNER: You'll never make money doing nothing.

ANDY: I've got a nice private enterprise on hand.

BANNER: We don't do too bad do we? I've made a packet and

you're not wanting. You know, mate, if they had people under thirty running this country we'd show a profit in no time at all.

ANDY: Yes, but if you're under thirty you've got to go around apologising for it—they don't realize that young people mature quicker these days.

BANNER: Yes, something to do with internal combustion I think.

[*Enter* NELL KALIN, *a prostitute.*]

NELL: Well—where've you been ?

ANDY: Waiting for you.

NELL: Take me for a drink.

BANNER: This young lady's face looks familiar. I'm sure I've seen it somewhere before.

NELL: That's his treat, isn't it ?

ANDY: Let me introduce you. This is Nell Kalin, one of the finest young girls in the land. Fair of face and soft of hand. Known far and wide throughout the city. A maiden sweet and wise and witty. Her help she never will refuse. . . .

NELL: Are you asking for a thick ear ?

ANDY: I'll give you one in a minute. . . .

BANNER: You're not polite, Andy.

NELL: He doesn't know the meaning of the word.

BANNER: Why do you bother with him, then ?

NELL: God alone knows and he won't split.

ANDY: Ah, now she knows I love her. . . .

NELL: The only thing he loves is himself and the money I earn for him. . . .

ANDY: That's a lie. My life's devoted to her, Banner. You know that ? I feed her, I clothe her, I look after her earnings. . . .

NELL: And spend them. . . .

ANDY: And every morning and every night I make sure she's in good working order.

NELL: He's trying to shock you.

BANNER: It takes a lot to shock me. I've been around.

NELL: And collected a few battle scars in the process too. . . .

BANNER: Yes, do you like 'em?

ANDY: This young man is shortly embarking on a great adventure, Nell. He's going round the world to seek his fortune.

NELL: Would you like a travelling companion?

BANNER: I wouldn't say no. . . .

NELL: There's no fortunes being made around here.

ANDY: I'm working on it.

NELL: And getting nowhere fast.

ANDY: These things take time. Just give me a couple of months and we'll be living like a king and queen. . . .

NELL: Yes—if I earn enough money. He's good for a laugh isn't he?

BANNER: Is he your manager?

NELL: That's the polite way of putting it.

ANDY: Now knock it off, Nell. Let's take Banner out for a drink.

NELL: Are you Peggy's brother?

BANNER: That's right.

NELL: Pleased to meet you.

BANNER: It's been charming.

ANDY: The beer's getting warm.

NELL: Who's paying for the drinks tonight?

BANNER: Me.

NELL: We'd better get going then.

ANDY: Where shall we go?

NELL: Somewhere where they don't know me.

ANDY: The Tavern?

NELL: Oh—Christ no. I always get thrown out of that hole. . . .

ANDY: There's a party on in the Fusiliers Arms.

BANNER: That's the place for us then. [*They go.*]

[*As* NELL, ANDY *and* BANNER *exit behind the house,* PEG *exits to kitchen.* JESSE *and* NORA *enter from the opposite side.*]

JESSE: Wakey, wakey! We're back.

NORA: You're just like your daughter, you are. Always making a row. [NORA *enters the house as* FRANK *enters from the kitchen.*]

JESSE: I'll wait here. You go and wake 'em up inside.

[NORA *and* FRANK, *inside the house.*]

NORA: Are you ready?

FRANK: Nearly. Should be a good party, Nora love.

NORA: I hope so.

FRANK: Well, it's a good job you're coming. I shouldn't be bothering otherwise. I usually end up in a corner on my own while she entertains everybody else.

NORA: Well, we can sit in a corner together, can't we?

[KIT *comes downstairs.* PEG *re-enters from the kitchen.*]

KIT: Well, are you fit?

FRANK: I've had to wait for you. Now it's your turn to wait for me.

KIT: Come on, Peg. We're not wanted here. Outcasts in our own home.

[PEG *and* KIT *leave the house.*]

KIT: Hello, Dad. That's a lovely flower you've got there.

JESSE: Do you like it then?

KIT: Beautiful. Where'd you get it from?

JESSE: Weaste Cemetery.

KIT: He hasn't changed a bit. D'you know, when I was a kid and he was out of work he used to bring my mother a bunch of flowers every day. And do you know where he got 'em from?

PEG: Pinched 'em out of the graveyard.

KIT: He was a villain then and he still is. Can I have this flower, Dad?

JESSE: Yes—there's plenty more where that came from.

KIT: No—you'd better keep it.

[*Inside the house.*]

FRANK: Were you the silly devil who paid her fine this morning?

NORA: Well somebody had to pay it—

FRANK: It needn't have been you!

NORA: Well she's my best friend.

FRANK: Here—[*He hands her two pounds. She refuses to take them.*] Take it. I'm not letting you pay her debts.

NORA: Keep it. We can have a good time on it tonight.

FRANK: Thanks.

[*Outside the house.*]

KIT: All quiet on the Western Front, isn't it? You two all right in there? What are you up to, Nora? Trying to violate my husband on the back doorstep.

NORA: Would I do a thing like that?

KIT: Just leave the man alone. He's weak enough as it is without you increasing the strain.

NORA: You ought to know me better than that.

KIT: That's the trouble. I know you only too well, and I know him, too. His head can be turned easy as a key in a lock. Women either throw themselves at him or run away screaming blue murder whenever they see his face. I've had similar trouble with him before so don't flatter yourself you're the first woman he's been unfaithful with, Nora, because you're not. Oh! I've seen him making love to the milkman's wife.

FRANK: You'd never catch me making love to the milkman's wife—the butcher's daughter wouldn't stand for that.

NORA: You daft thing.

KIT: Are you listening, Peg? You'll know what to expect when you get married. You'll soon find out that the national sport of Englishmen is hypocrisy.

FRANK: Stop carrying on—you're already entertaining half the street.

KIT: It's a pity our neighbours haven't got something better to do than mind everybody else's business. Are you listening? Can you hear?

JESSE: Stop making a public exhibition of yourself.

KIT: It's a public place. I'll do what I like in it. Are you having a good look?

JESSE: You know what she needs, don't you. A good thrashing. That's what she's gone short of.

FRANK: Are you coming or aren't you?

KIT: I'll come when I'm ready.

FRANK: You'll come now or not at all.

KIT: Don't order me about.

FRANK: You'll come now.

JESSE: Let's all go and have a drink and hope to die stone cold drunk. Ta'ra, Peg, you mind the house till we get back.

[*They go.* PEG *is alone. A snazzily dressed boy enters. He approaches her.*]

LOLL: Excuse me, miss, but I'm a stranger round here. Could you direct me to your house.

PEG: Buzz off.

LOLL: Yes, it is a nice night isn't it? Still, it's a special night isn't it—St. Valentine's. Got many Valentine cards?

PEG: Hundreds—

LOLL: How's this one sound—

> My heart is like a cabbage
> Divided into two.
> The leaves I give to others
> The heart I give to you.

PEG: Here's a penny. Go and sing in the next street.

LOLL: Live round here?

PEG: I live here.

LOLL: Oh! How long has it been condemned?

PEG: Somebody ought to condemn you.

LOLL: My mother maintains that someone will one of these days. What's your name?

PEG: Peggy.

LOLL: Pleased to meet you. My name's Loll Stephens. Now I hope you don't mind me talking to you like this, but I just like talking to people and I haven't been in this place long so I don't know many. Will you show me the local beauty spots?

PEG: I am the local beauty spot.

LOLL: Well, let's get a closer look.

PEG: You do it with your eyes not your hands.

LOLL: Girls are more co-operative where I come from.

PEG: Then you want to go back there. Do you come from Scotland?

LOLL: That's right. From Glasgow, the greatest city in the world.

PEG: Why'd you leave it then?

LOLL: Well, you know how it is. By the time I was old enough for my mother to be able to stand the sight of me, I couldn't stand the sight of her. So I hopped it. This isn't such a bad place to be though. I imagine you could get very fond of it from a distance.

PEG: What are you doing down here?

LOLL: Looking around, chicksie, just looking around. Maybe I'll stay, maybe I won't. Who cares? I don't care.

PEG: What do you really do?

LOLL: I've come down here to study textiles and things at the college. I'm going to be a dress designer.

PEG: A what?

LOLL: A dress designer. There's nothing wrong in that, is there?

PEG: No.

LOLL: My old lady thinks I'm mad because I won't stay at home like the rest of 'em. But there's hardly enough work to go round there. Half the fellers I left school with still haven't found steady jobs yet, you know, and I'm not going to be pushed into any old job.

PEG: So you've come down here—

LOLL: Yes, I've always wanted to do something like this any-way—I went to art school for a couple of months after I finished with day school, but my mother made me chuck it. No money in it, she said. My old lady isn't one for dreams.

PEG: Isn't she?

LOLL: No. Is yours?

PEG: She always believes in having a go. Your family in Scotland?

LOLL: Yes—my mother and my sister.

PEG: No dad?

LOLL: He's dead.

PEG: What's your sister's name?

LOLL: Charlotte the Harlot the cowpunchers' whore.

PEG: Shut up.

LOLL: And I've got a brother too but he's a sad case. Tied to his mother's apron strings. It's worrying really. There are times when he treats her like a normal woman. But she hates me, thinks I'm a rogue. Mind you, I've not got much time for her either. We never got on well together. Hey! Did your mother ever tell you what it meant if a young man asked her to go for a walk in the park.

PEG: She knew what it meant all right?

LOLL: But I'll bet it didn't stop her from going all the same. Come on.

PEG: No.

LOLL: All right then, let's stay here. Indulge in a bit of social chit chat.

PEG: Oh well—if you want to waste your time.

LOLL: I've plenty of time to waste.

[*Music from a local pub is heard.*]

LOLL: Sounds as if someone's enjoying themselves. You're not much fun are you? Come on, relax. Let's get your clothes off, kid, and have some fun.

PEG: You'd get a shock if I did take my clothes off.

LOLL: Why, are you really a boy?

PEG: Oh, I'm a girl all right.

LOLL: Well, prove it, then.

[*A train passes through the station.*]

PEG: Wonder where that was going.

LOLL: Why don't you get on a train with me—we could go anywhere.

PEG: You need money.

LOLL: Good-looking girl like you needn't go short of a few coppers. Give me a kiss.

PEG: Go away.

LOLL: Come on, I'll take you for a ride in my car.

PEG: Have you got one?

LOLL: Of course.

PEG: Where is it?

LOLL: Parked round the corner.

PEG: What colour?

LOLL: Sky blue pink with a yellow border.

PEG: Sounds a bit vulgar.

LOLL: It's like me. Vulgar but comfortable.

PEG: Where would we be without imagination?

LOLL: Don't you believe me?

PEG: Do I heck.

LOLL: There's nothing wrong with the odd fib—lying's a very bad virtue I always think. See that star up there. That's the evening star.

PEG: How do you know?

LOLL: My grandad told me. Old feller used to be a sailor. Taught me the name of every star in the sky.

PEG: And that's the evening star.

[*He kisses her.*]

You cheeky devil. Who do you think you are, going round kissing people you hardly know. Clear off.

LOLL: Now you like it really.

PEG: Some men don't half fancy their little selves.

LOLL: Don't provoke me.

PEG: Go on.

LOLL [*he takes hold of her*]: You know what your trouble is? You've got come-to-bed eyes.

PEG: Help. [*She frees herself.*]

LOLL: Relax, kid, relax.

PEG: You leave me alone. [*She is annoyed but not a bit frightened.*]

LOLL: Well, there it is—defeat. A rough diamond like me from the Gorbals beaten not by a bruiser but a sweet little girl like you. A sweet little girl with a neat little figure—thirty-six hip, I'd say—twenty-one waist if I'm not mistaken and a thirty-eight bust.

PEG: Thirty-six. Disappointed?

LOLL: No. Suits me. Give me quality over quantity every time.

PEG: Are you going now?

LOLL: Come on, I'll buy you a cup of tea down the road.

PEG: Behave then.

LOLL: Good as gold. I always behave.

PEG: I've got to be home early.

LOLL: I'll have you on the front door step in good time.

PEG: I'll get into trouble if I'm late.

LOLL: If you get into trouble, Peg, just tell Loll and I'll keep right out of the way.

SCENE TWO

ANDY, NELL *and* BANNER *come on dancing and singing. They are all slightly drunk.*

NELL: You'd better get him to bed.

ANDY: How about it, Banner boy?

BANNER: I'm not tired.

ANDY: Now come on—beddybyes. . . .

BANNER: Lay off, will you. . . .

ANDY: Now then. . . .

BANNER: You think I'm drunk, don't you?

NELL: He's hardly had any beer.

ANDY: He never could take it. Come on, pick your feet up, sonny Jim. . . .

NELL: If this is what half a dozen black and tans do for him, I'd hate to let him loose on a bottle of gin. . . .

ANDY [*dancing* BANNER *towards the house*]: Come on inside.

BANNER: Hey! Hey! Be careful. You'll have the neighbours talking. [*He throws* ANDY *aside and enters the house.*] I am perfectly all right.

[*The others follow.* BANNER *sprawls down on the couch.*]

NELL: It's cold in here.

BANNER: I'll tell you what to do. Get a piece of chalk and draw yourself a fire. Oh! I feel terrible. Fancy spending all that money, just to make yourself feel sick.

NELL: Well, go to sleep.

[*She starts to fumble with his tie.*]

BANNER: Hey! What're you doing? Leave me alone. . . .

ANDY: Oh, shut up, before. . . .

BANNER: D'you want a fight? Is that what you're after?

NELL: Oh, I'm going outside. He's getting on my nerves.

ANDY: You stay where you are.

NELL: Don't start on me.

BANNER: Don't go yet.

ANDY: You get some kip. It's been a long night.

BANNER: Have a cigarette then—go on.

NELL: That's a nice case.

BANNER: That's gold.

NELL: I know it is.

BANNER: Pure gold.

NELL: Not bad is it?

BANNER: Pure gold. The best for the best. Cost me a small fortune.

NELL: I bet it did.

BANNER: Not that I miss it, mind you. There's plenty of money knocking about if you know where to look.

NELL: You've spent enough tonight.

ANDY: You weren't backwards in coming forwards to help him.

NELL: He enjoyed it.

BANNER: 'Course I enjoyed it. She's a nice girl.

ANDY: 'Course she's a nice girl. Get some kip.

BANNER [*pulling out a wad of notes*]: Eh, look at that! Stacks of it. I'm not behind the door, you know.

ANDY: Who's he kidding?

BANNER: I tell you, Nell, if you're smart you can do anything.

ANDY: Isn't he the clever one?

BANNER: I used to be handy with me fists—I still am if it comes to that—but when I was a pro I made a fortune—

ANDY: Who are you kidding!

BANNER: And I made it with these. You just get stuck in and you're made.

NELL: I've never been all that interested in boxing. Were you good, then?

BANNER: I wasn't too bad. Made a good living.

ANDY: While it lasted.

BANNER: I chucked the game, you know. It didn't chuck me.

ANDY: What about that boy in Liverpool? You didn't beat him, did you?

BANNER: I've beaten better men than him.

ANDY: But you didn't beat him.

BANNER: I was overtrained. That's all, I was overtrained.

ANDY: Don't try and kid me, sonny. Kid the old man and kid your old Dad about it but don't try it on me. I know better. We're two of a kind, me and you, Banner. Big in a little way. Stick your money back in your pocket, you might be needing it one day. Fool 'em all and kid 'em all but don't try and kid me, because I'm one of the kidders myself, boy.

NELL: Yes. And your star-spangled moment's gone for good.

ANDY: Maybe it has but I can still show 'em a thing or two if I felt like it.

NELL: Then why don't you try? Are you scared?

ANDY: I'm scared of nothing.

NELL: Then why don't you have a go? You're all talk.

ANDY: I might do, one of these days.

NELL: You might.

ANDY: I might. That'd give you a shock wouldn't it?

NELL: Yes, it would. You're always talking about this act you used to do. Why don't you do something about it instead of hanging about here? We could team up properly.

ANDY: You're not in the same class as me.

NELL: You're no Fred Astaire.

ANDY: Ah! Knock it off! Let's get moving. He'll be all right. Till his folks get back.

[ANDY *and* NELL *leave the house.* KIT *and* JESSE *return from the party.*]

JESSE and KIT [*singing*]: I should like it all over again
                          I should like it all over again
                          Though it might sound absurd
                          Upon my word!
                          I should like it all over again.

ANDY: You sound as if you've had a good time.

KIT: We always have a good time.

[*She dances in the street and calls out to the neighbours.*]

Hello, Mrs. Briggs! It's me again.

JESSE: It's been very nice, very nice indeed. I've still got some of this brandy left. Your son brought me this, Kit. Who'll join me in a little drink?

ANDY: Not for me, thanks. . . .

KIT: Give it here. . . .

JESSE [*dodging her grasping hands*]: You pay for your own. . . . Nell?

KIT: Old misery.

[*She prowls the street, knowing that the neighbours' eyes are on her and performing especially for them in defiance and contempt.* KIT's *next four speeches are, in fact,* ad libs, *and must not intrude on the main dialogue.*]

NELL: No thanks. . . .

JESSE: You're quite right to keep away from it. Drink's a terrible thing. I'll be glad when I've had enough of it. Here we are then. I offer you a toast, ladies and gentlemen. A toast to celebrate the homecoming of this young man. Wake up, son, I'm talking to you. . . .

KIT: My son. That's my son, Mrs. Wilton, peeping at me from behind your bedroom curtains. Ah, get back to it, you old bat!

JESSE: Listen to me, son. There's a lot of people who're jealous of your youth and they'll try and take it away from you but you hang on to it. It's a wonderful thing. . . .

KIT: A wonderful thing! Hallo, Mrs. Middleton. It's me again, drunk as usual. Dancing in public again. She's a devil, isn't she? Ah! Get back to bed, you old witch.

JESSE: Bread, beer and youth! The jewels of life! God bless us! [*He drinks.*]

KIT: The jewels of life. . . .

ANDY [*taking the bottle from* JESSE *and putting his arms around* NELL]: I'll give you another one. Here's health to all those we love, here's health to all those that love us, and here's health to all those that love them that love those that love us. AMEN.

KIT [*through his speech*]: All those we love. They're a lovely couple, aren't they? A lovely couple.

JESSE: Now give us my brandy back.

ANDY: And now it's time we were in bed. . . .

[ANDY *and* NELL *link arms and make to go off home.*]

KIT: Hey you, if you see my husband on your way home just tell him I'm waiting, will you?

NELL: Has he left you at last?

KIT: He is escorting Nora home.

JESSE: She doesn't know her way round yet.

KIT: No. She's only lived here for the last twenty years.

ANDY: She's getting jealous.

KIT: I am and I don't mind admitting it either. Frank's a good man.

NELL: What will you do if he doesn't come back?

KIT: He'll come back all right. I'll say one thing for him. He's stood by me like a rock through all the trouble he didn't have until he married me.

ANDY: Well, if he does go, remember me. I'll keep you warm in winter.

KIT: I'll remember.

NELL: So will I. Get going, you.

[*Exit* ANDY *and* NELL. KIT *enters the house.*]

KIT: What's up with him? He's got a face as long as a penny fiddle.

BANNER: I'm thinking.

KIT: What with? [*She takes the cigarette from him.*] You're too young to smoke. [*She smokes it herself.*]

BANNER: And you're old enough to know better.

KIT: A woman is as old as she looks.

JESSE: And you look about ninety.

KIT: And I feel ninety—it's not every day a woman comes face to face with a twenty-two-year-old son.

JESSE: Well, it comes to us all sooner or later.

KIT: It needn't come as such a shock. Still, I'm not dead yet, am I? There's more life in me than there is in a lot around here.

JESSE: Eh! Did you see this box he bought for Peggy?

KIT: What is it?

JESSE: Music box—

BANNER [*as his mother starts to handle it roughly*]: Give it here. You've got to be careful with it. It's delicate. [*He opens the lid. Music.*]

KIT: I've never heard that tune before.

BANNER: It's modern. . . .

KIT: It's nice, isn't it? Needs a bit of life putting into it though. Let's have a dance. Come on.

[KIT *pulls* BANNER *off the couch and swings him round.*]

[BANNER *breaks away from* KIT *and bangs down the music box lid.*]

You're not very sociable are you?

BANNER: I'm tired. I'm going to bed.

KIT: It doesn't take much to wear you out does it?

BANNER: I've been travelling all day. . . .

KIT: Sitting on your backside in a first class carriage. . . .

BANNER: I'm tired, that's all. I just want to go to bed.

KIT: You can go to hell for all I care.

JESSE [*as* BANNER *goes*]: Good night, son. He hasn't been home five minutes and you're picking a fight with him already. You don't seem happy unless you're fighting with someone.

KIT: I take after you.

JESSE: Less of the old buck.

KIT: Don't talk to me like that. How old do you think I am?

JESSE: I sometimes wonder. The older you get the dafter you get.

KIT: If you want to preach sermons go and do it in the church —not here.

JESSE: I wish I was able. I'd give you a good hiding. . . . Do you want to drive the lad away again?

KIT: If he's going he'll go. Makes no difference what I do.

JESSE: You're his mother.

KIT: I haven't forgotten that by a long chalk. He doesn't seem to remember much about it, though. All the time he's been away he's written to me once.

JESSE: He's young. Kids are too busy to sit down and start writing letters. You ought to be more sympathetic.

KIT: I haven't forgotten what it's like to be young, Dad.

JESSE: Well, you're still young.

KIT: I'm old enough to know that what people want to do they'll do and there's nothing you can say to stop 'em. Anything I've done, I've done with my eyes wide open and there's no one to blame but myself. Right?

JESSE: Right. Your mother wouldn't like to see some of the things you do now, Kathleen.

KIT: She didn't like to see some of the things I did when she was alive.

JESSE: Many's the time she cried over the way you treated her.

KIT: And many's the time she cried over the way you treated her.

JESSE: That was different.

KIT: You led her a hell of a life.

JESSE: She never complained. And anyway she gave as good as she got. She could look after herself, could your mother. A very independent woman. I'll admit we had some rare barnies and we did terrible things to each other but we were still fond of each other. . . .

KIT: Well, it's the same with me and Frank, we have a go every now and again, but it doesn't mean much in the long run.

JESSE: Don't be too sure, love. You push him too far sometimes.

KIT: Hey! I'm not as bad as all that.

JESSE: You'll drive your husband up the wall if you're not careful.

KIT: It doesn't take much to drive him anywhere. And it doesn't take much to drive him back either.

JESSE: One of these days he won't come back.

KIT: Think so?

JESSE: I do.

KIT: He won't find another one like me anywhere.

JESSE: And he'll thank God for that too.

KIT: His other women come and his other women go but his wife goes on forever—you silly old devil—it's time you stopped worrying about me and got on with enjoying your life—there's not much of it left, you know. . . .

JESSE: I sometimes think that's a good thing too. . . .

KIT [*picking up the box*]: It's a nice box Banner bought for Peg, isn't it? Looks expensive too. [*Inspecting it.*] Made in Switzerland. D'you remember that one me and Frank bought her when she was a kid? I always remember that. Frank had just come out of the army and we hadn't got two ha'pennies for a penny between us. We turned this city upside down trying to find her a music box for Christmas. . . .

JESSE: Aye, and when she got it what happened? She played it for five minutes and then threw it in the corner.

KIT: Ah, well, that's the way kids are. Are you warm enough?

JESSE: I'm off to bed in a minute.

KIT: Your flower is starting to wilt a bit.

JESSE: It's like me. It needs a drink.

KIT: Finish your brandy off then—

JESSE: It's good stuff this—puts life into you. . . .

KIT: Do you think Sonny Jim's all right up there? He's very quiet.

JESSE: Give him a shout. He might like a cup of tea.

KIT: Banner! Banner! Are you awake?

JESSE [*as no answer comes*]: Dead to the world.

KIT: He enjoyed the party anyway.

JESSE: So did I. So did everybody.

KIT: Until you started to sing.

JESSE: There's nothing wrong with my voice. If they'd had television when I was a youth I'd have been a star over-night with my golden tonsils and good looks. Remember the song I sang at your wedding. . . .

[*He sings.*]

> I'll take you home again, Kathleen,
> To where the fields are fresh and green
> To where your heart has ever been
> Since first you came my blushing bride.
> The roses all have left your cheeks
> I've watched them fade away and die
> Your voice is sad when 'ere you speak
> And tears bedim your loving eyes . . . [*etc. etc.*]

[FRANK *enters and interrupts the song:*]

FRANK: You two still keeping the party going? Enjoy your-self—?

KIT: I always enjoy myself. So did you, by the looks of things. See Nora home all right? Is she safe?

JESSE: Well, I'll love you and leave you.

FRANK: Don't let her scare you off.

JESSE: It takes more than her to put the scares up me.

[*He dances with them both and sings.*]

Oh, I don't care if she's skin and bone and half a mile round the Hippodrome. . . .

FRANK [*disentangling himself*]: Hey! Now then—you watch it. Be careful. Remember what happened last time. You go upstairs and get your beauty sleep.

JESSE: Oh well. Good night.

FRANK: He's as lively as a kid, the old devil.

KIT: Yes.

FRANK: Banner home?

KIT: He's in bed.

FRANK: It's nice to have the family together again, isn't it?

KIT: I'll bet he doesn't stay here five minutes.

FRANK: He might—if you asked him to. You never know. He might decide that there's no place like home.

KIT: There's no place like this home anyway.

FRANK: I'm tired.

KIT: Let's go to bed then.

FRANK: Where are my slippers?

[*She gets them for him.*]

KIT: Where the hell did you get that hat from?

FRANK: I treated myself to it last week. Don't you like it?

KIT: Let's have a look at it—old big head.

FRANK: I thought I looked rather smart myself.

KIT: You don't half fancy yourself. Makes you look about fourteen.

FRANK: Do you fancy me then?

KIT: I've always fancied you.

FRANK: You've never been able to resist me, have you? Overwhelmed by my devastating charm.

KIT: The smell of your hair cream, more like.

FRANK: Ashes of roses. Sixpence a bottle.

KIT: Sixpence a gallon, you mean.

FRANK: We were a smart couple in those days.

KIT: We still are.

FRANK: Give me a kiss.

[*They kiss.*]

KIT: You'd better not let Nora see us.

FRANK: How do you mean?

KIT: She might not like it.

FRANK: Are you jealous?

KIT: Have I cause to be?

FRANK: Ask yourself.

KIT: Tell me one thing. What do you see in Nora?

FRANK: Don't talk daft. Let's go to bed.

KIT: Don't think you're fooling me. I don't miss a thing.

FRANK: I've nothing to hide.

KIT: It's a good job because you're no good at hiding anything. Well, when are you going?

FRANK: You'd be in a sorry state if I did go.

KIT: Don't let me stop you. I can get by.

FRANK: I wish that was true.

KIT: It is—I won't be a burden on you.

FRANK: Look, Kit, you're my wife. I married you and I don't object to looking after you. . . .

KIT: That's very kind of you I'm sure. . . .

FRANK: But I'm fed up with the way you carry on. It's about time you chucked this riotous living and calmed down a bit. . . .

KIT: While you fiddle with Nora on the sly? Not likely. I'm not being second best to anybody—least of all Nora. If I'm your wife you should treat me like your wife.

FRANK: Since when have you ever behaved like one?

KIT: Aw, stop nagging me. You're like an old woman.

FRANK: Me nagging? You've never stopped nagging me since the day we got married. Even when I was in the army you used to write me nagging letters. You couldn't even let me enjoy the war in peace.

KIT: When I married you there was only one thing certain about the future—there was going to be a lot of it.

FRANK: There's been more than enough for me.

KIT: Then you know what to do about it, don't you?

FRANK: I've done it before.

KIT: Yes, and you've always come back.

FRANK: Don't shout at me.

JESSE [*from upstairs*]: Will you two be quiet. You're making enough noise to wake my wife up and she's been dead for twenty years. Keep your woman in order, Frank. And for God's sake let's have a bit of peace and quiet as Billy Butterworth said when he threw his mother-in-law behind the fire.

FRANK: The day you die I'm going to have you embalmed, buried and cremated.

KIT: That's right love, take no chances. Where's Peg got to?

FRANK: She should be here.

KIT: I bet she's gone out somewhere. The little devil.

FRANK: You ought to take more notice of her. Have a serious talk with her.

KIT: And make a complete fool of myself? Not likely. I remember the night before I married you my mother had a serious talk with me about what to expect from married life, huh! I was sixteen, you were eighteen and Banner had been browning nicely in the oven for nearly three months.

FRANK: Accidents happen.

KIT: Especially to me.

FRANK: I don't want the same thing happening to Peg. She knows too much as it is.

KIT: It's not what she knows that should worry you—it's how she found out in the first place.

[PEG *and* LOLL *dance on.*]

So you've come back, have you? And where do you think you've been?

PEG: Coming.

KIT: And not before time either. Good evening, young man, where are you from and what do you do? My name's Kathleen, who the hell are you?

LOLL: Loll Stephens. Pleased to meet you.

KIT: Pleased to meet you. This is Mr. Fresko, my husband!

FRANK: Scotch lad?

LOLL: That's right.

FRANK: Working down here?

LOLL: Not exactly.

KIT: He's one of the glorious unemployed like me.

LOLL: That's right, missis. And if things get any better in this country there'll soon be enough unemployment for everybody.

KIT: True enough.

FRANK: You've got yourself a right smart Alec here, haven't you?

KIT: She's wise. The night I met you the moon was a damn sight brighter than I was.

PEG: Don't talk like that. You'll give people the wrong impression.

KIT: Where've you been?

PEG: Just walking about. You'd better be going, Loll, or you'll miss the last bus back to town.

KIT: Don't worry about the buses, Loll. Kip down here on the couch.

LOLL: No. I'd better go. My landlady isn't keen on her lodgers staying out all night. She likes to know what they're getting up to.

KIT: Suit yourself. I'm off to bed. I'll see you again then, I suppose. You lock up down here, Frank. We don't want burglars, do we? Mind you, if they ever broke into this house I'd give them a hand looking for something worth pinching.

[KIT *goes upstairs.*]

LOLL: Good night, Mr. Fresko.

FRANK: Good night.

PEG: I'll see you to the corner.

FRANK: Don't be long, Peggy.

PEG: I won't.

[PEG *and* LOLL *walk to the lamp-post and kiss good night.*]

FRANK: Look at them two. I'll bet they haven't known each other five minutes. You've got to laugh at 'em. And her upstairs too—makes you wonder. Mind you, the more you see of some people the more it makes you believe in birth control.

Curtain

Act Two

The time is the following Saturday, early in the day. The market off-stage is in full swing, and the sounds of it drift across the set. The house has become a sort of canteen for the market folk. PEG keeps taking tea out to the stalls. People pass across the stage, coming and going to market. A PORTER carts provisions from a store behind the house to a stall off the other side of the stage. The setting is a backwater attached to the market. NELL solicits discreetly by the lamp-post. ANDY keeps an eye on her. NORA sits outside the house drinking tea with JESSE. ENA and LENA cross on their way to the market.

NORA: Is that the new baby, Ena?

ENA: Don't wake him.

ANDY [*peering into the pram*]: Funny looking little devil, isn't he? Looks like one of Frank's shrunken heads.

JESSE [*dangling one of* FRANK'S *furry toy monkeys over the pram*]: Give him one of these to play with.

ANDY: You can't tell the difference, can you?

LENA: It costs a fortune to keep kids quiet, doesn't it?

JESSE: It costs more to amuse the child than it did to educate the father.

NELL: How many kids have you got now, missus?

LENA: Twelve.

ENA: It's a lot, isn't it? Still—it'll be all right when they're all working.

NORA [*as* ANDY *prods the baby*]: Be careful, you'll wake him.

ENA: You like kids don't you, Nora?

NORA: Who doesn't?

LENA: You'd be surprised. You must regret never having any of your own.

NORA: Well, I look at life this road, love. What you never have you never miss.

ENA: Well, I've got twelve and I wouldn't be without one of them. It's my husband's birthday on Monday, Nora. I'm trying to find him a present. What do you think he'd like?

NORA: Shall I tell you? Never mind what he'd like, love, buy him a tie. I've got just the thing on the stall. Pure silk. Half a crown to you. And I've got a lovely nylon nightdress, hardly been worn—

ENA: Can you see me wearing that in bed with my husband...?

JESSE: Like throwing petrol on a blazing fire.

ENA: Don't be so saucy.

[ENA, LENA and NORA *go off to* NORA'S *stall*.]

JESSE: I think I'll go and relieve Frank. They were going to let him know about giving him a stall licence this morning.

PEG: Think he'll get it?

JESSE: I don't know, love. I hope so. It'll give him a better living than he gets from the suitcase.

PEG: A bit more money wouldn't hurt in this house.

JESSE: You can say that again. I'll take him some more shrunken heads.

[JESSE *goes out of the house and crosses to relieve* FRANK.]

JESSE [*to* NELL]: You'll have Mr. Butler after you.

NELL: I can run.

JESSE: Give us a kiss on tick.

NELL: The last man died.

JESSE: Can you recognize him among this lot? Look at that, eh? Spitting image of your grandmother. [*He holds up a shrunken head.*]

[JESSE *exits and* NELL *moves away.*]

ANDY: Where do you think you're going?

NELL: I'm fed up with hanging about here. There's nothing doing at all.

ANDY: Give the place time to warm up.

[FRANK *enters from the market*.]

FRANK: How's trade?

ANDY: Bloody awful.

FRANK [*entering the house*]: Put her on the hire purchase, then.

ANDY: Not on my Nelly.

[FRANK *enters the house*.]

PEG: What about the licence, Dad? Did you get it?

FRANK: Did I hell. The bastards turned it down. They're granting no more stall licences for the market. They're trying to close it down.

PEG: Don't you let them push you out.

FRANK: Fat chance I have of stopping them.

[PEG *exits with a tray of tea cups.* KIT *is coming down the stairs*.]

KIT: Hello, loverlips.

FRANK: You were late in last night.

KIT: Banner took me to a new club that's opened in Manchester—they didn't close the bar till two o'clock.

FRANK: Banner ought to have more sense.

KIT: We enjoyed it—you should've come with us.

FRANK: I wasn't asked.

KIT: Oh! Well, that's the way it goes. What sort of weather is it this morning?

FRANK: Where are you going?

KIT: Out.

FRANK: Up, down and out. Peggy's getting just like you—she's hardly ever in this house—she only uses it for sleeping and eating—it's not a canteen, you know.

KIT: It's a very nice house, love, and I'm very fond of it. I'd better put my scarf on—it looks as if it might rain. Will you lend me half a dollar?

FRANK: No, I won't.

KIT: Go on—half a crown. I'll give it you back as soon as I can.

FRANK: I'm not giving you money to go boozing with.

KIT: You miserable old dog! How mean can you get?

FRANK: I'm not being mean, but all these half crowns and two bob pieces that you borrow mount up. It's about time somebody around here started being a bit more careful with the family finances and thought a bit more about the future. . . .

KIT: Oh! Listen to it. What's biting you this morning? You look more miserable than usual.

FRANK: The council won't give me a licence to put up a stall in the market—

KIT: Oh! So it's back to the old suitcase and the street corners, is it?

FRANK: Yes—right back.

KIT: Never mind, lover, we won't be any the worse off than we are now.

FRANK: Don't be too sure. The market's closing up. They're getting rid of blokes like me. If I'd had any sense ten years ago, I'd have checked out of it and started up a proper business of my own.

KIT: I'll get a job. If we both worked hard together we could save the money and buy a lot of things.

FRANK: I wish I could believe that.

KIT: But you can. I'm fed up with doing nothing. I'm dying to get back to work.

FRANK: You'll never stick it. Why don't you face the bloody truth—you don't like hard work.

KIT: I don't mind work. I've had four jobs already this year. How's that for enthusiasm?

FRANK: And how long have they lasted?

KIT: Well, it's not my fault, Frank. I get a job and I like the money. I like the people and I don't complain about the work but as soon as some snotty nosed little foreman in a brown overall walks up to me and starts telling me what I can do and what I can't do, that's my lot! I just can't stick it—I'm out. . . .

FRANK: That's what I mean—you never stick it. As long as you're enjoying yourself you don't care about anything else.

KIT: But that's not true, Frank. I just don't like being pushed around.

FRANK: We'll end up by being pushed in the workhouse—we're not kids any more, Kit. We ought to be thinking about the future.

KIT: We're not old age pensioners yet!

FRANK: It'll be too late to worry when we are.

KIT: Well, it's too soon to worry now. I can't be bothered with things that might happen. I'll face 'em when they comes and not before. Now lend me some money and I'll get going—

FRANK: It's as easy as that, isn't it?

KIT: Look, Frank, don't expect me to start thinking twenty years ahead of myself because I'm not going to do it. It's a waste of time. It does no good at all, and if you won't lend me half a dollar I'll just have to go and find someone who will, won't I?

FRANK: Yes, there'll always be some mug willing to buy you a pint, won't there? Well, this mug's finished emptying his pockets for your benefit—he's had enough.

KIT: If you begrudge supporting me, Frank, I don't mind— just sling your hook. Take your things out of my father's house. Go and move in with Nora—see if she treats you any better.

FRANK: She couldn't treat me any worse.

KIT: Oh! Don't stand there looking like a wet week. Cheer up for God's sake.

[*She leaves the house and grabs* PEGGY.]

Hey! you, come here. Where's your purse ?

PEG: Are you on the cadge again ?

KIT [*looking through the purse*]: Let's see how much you've got. . . .

PEG: That's not my money. It belongs to my dad.

KIT: Oh! Well, he won't miss it. Tell him I've borrowed five bob—ta'ra, love, you're my best pal. [*She strolls off, waving to* NELL.] Hallo, Nell . . . [*Exit.*]

[JESSE *returns.*]

JESSE: Are you still here? If you stand there much longer you'll take root.

[*A* BEARDED PROPHET *with a banner enters, distributing pamphlets.*]

Hey! Can a man with a beard tell a barefaced lie ? Go on, have a go, Nell. Lovely girl, sir. Worth her weight in gold.

NELL: All on your own, love ?

JESSE: Always remember, sir, good things come in small bundles.

PROPHET: So does poison. [*He exits.*]

PEG: It's going to rain.

JESSE: Do my marrows good.

FRANK: Who's looking after my case ?

JESSE: Nora.

[FRANK *leaves the house. Thunder is in the air. It gets darker. Everybody scuttles for shelter.* ENA *and* LENA *enter.*]

LENA: Have you got everything, love ? You know what you're like. Did you buy some apples off that chap ?

ENA: Got a bag full here.

LENA: Let's have a look. I thought so. They're rotten.

ENA: Are they ?

LENA: Why'd you buy a pound of rotten apples ?

ENA: They are a bit bad, aren't they?

LENA: They must have seen you coming.

ENA: Oh, it is a twist, isn't it? Look at 'em. Half of 'em are green and the rest are like putty. There's no enjoyment in them things, is there? Look at them. Two bob a pound they were too. Oh! I hate twisters. I've a good mind to take 'em back. . . .

LENA: You'd be within your rights.

ENA: You can't afford to waste money on things like that, can you?

LENA: It's coming on to rain.

ENA: They'd take money from a blind man, they would. I've never known such in all my life. It's not the first time either. They've played this trick on me before. They think I'm soft or something. . . . Rain or no rain, I've a good mind to go back there and ram these down that chap's throat, one by one—worms an' all.

LENA: Just look at that girl. I don't know how she's got the cheek to show her face in public.

NELL [*perfectly aware that they are talking about her*]: Have you seen enough?

LENA: Oh! Isn't she rude?

NELL: Do I owe you anything?

ENA [*to* NELL]: Not that we know of. [*To* LENA] Like mother like daughter. Dead brassy.

LENA: Some people don't know when to feel ashamed of themselves. Just look at her. Modern youth. That's the sort of thing we've been paying rates and taxes for all these years.

ANDY: I'll tell you what you get for your rates and taxes: the Hallé Orchestra and your dustbins emptied once a week.

NELL: And a small fortune in family allowances.

ANDY: And enough orange juice to feed a football team.

NELL: Didn't your Mum ever tell you it's rude to stare?

LENA: Don't you start preaching good manners at us.

NELL: Oh! Belt up, you old witch.

LENA: Isn't she hardfaced?

ENA: You've respect for nothing.

NELL: I've none for you.

LENA: Ignore her. She's not worth bothering with.

NELL: Ah, go back to hell where you come from.

ENA: Cheeky little bitch.

LENA: She takes after her mother. That woman was just the same. She'd go to bed with anybody for a shilling for the gas and five woodbines.

ANDY: They're still talking about you.

NELL: They've got to have somebody to talk about. Small things amuse small minds.

ENA: I remember her mother well. She was a devil for the men. She used to have digs in my father's house during the war. I'll never forget one night when a chap she was knocking about with run off and pinched all her clothes.

LENA: Aye! I'll bet she didn't miss 'em for a week.

NELL: Have you done?

LENA: Are you talking to us?

NELL: Have you finished pulling me to pieces?

LENA: Don't talk to us like that.

NELL: Just be quiet, you old witch, or somebody'll cut your tongue off one of these days.

ENA: I'll witch you in a minute if you're not careful.

LENA: Come on. It's clearing up now—

ENA: She needs a good talking to.

LENA: Let's go and see about your apples.

ENA: My what?

LENA: Your apples.

ENA: What's wrong with them? Oh! aye—I must be going doolally.

[*They exit.*]

[BANNER *leaves the house. He taps* ANDY *on the shoulder.*]

BANNER: Hey up! Sergeant-major.

MAUREEN [*coming on to meet him*]. I'm sorry I'm late.

BANNER: That's all right, love. [*He takes her arm and they go off.*]

NELL: I could wring their silly necks.

ANDY: Don't take it to heart, Nell. . . .

NELL: It's all very well for you to talk. You don't have to put up with it. You don't have to stand about all day like this.

ANDY: I am standing about.

NELL: Like piffy on a rock bun.

ANDY: Like piffy on a rock bun.

NELL: While silly old women like that sneer at you. I'm fed up with it. I'm fed up to the back teeth and I'm going. I've had just about as much as I can take.

ANDY: Where are you going?

NELL: Back to London. I could be earning a steady fifty a week there, instead of ten if I'm lucky in this hole.

ANDY: You can't go away now—

NELL: I can go when I please and I'm going now.

ANDY: Good times are coming.

NELL: I've heard it all before.

ANDY: It's true this time. Just hold on a bit longer and we'll be rolling.

NELL: I'm not in the mood for funny stories.

ANDY: Stay with me, Nell.

NELL: Why?

ANDY: I need you.

NELL: For what?

ANDY: To take care of me.

NELL: Perhaps one day someone will start taking care of me.

ANDY: I do my best, Nell. I've got big plans for us two.

NELL: Oh! Let me go. I've got better things to do than hang around here.

ANDY: I promise you, Nell.

NELL: Pull the other leg—it's got bells on it.

ANDY: Cross my heart. I'm going to get a job. I know a bloke

who's opened a new club in Manchester and he's looking
for new acts and I'm going to see if he could use us two as a
double act.

NELL: Are you serious ?

ANDY: I'm always serious where you're concerned. I don't
want you walking the streets for the rest of your life. I
want you for myself sometime and this is the way to do it.
You can dance can't you—

NELL: I worked in that club in London. I didn't take my
clothes off though. But it wasn't what you'd call dancing.
I just stonked around to the music.

ANDY: Well, that's a start anyway. You don't have to be good
—you just have to look good. You can get away with anything if you do it in style.

NELL: D'you think we could do it ?

ANDY: Sure we can do it. We'd be a sensation.

NELL: I can do classical stuff. My mam wanted me to be a
ballet dancer.

ANDY: Well, ballet will give the act a bit of class. With your
classical stuff and my acrobatics—[*He turns a somersault.*]—
we'll be well away. You do want to try it ?

NELL: 'Course I do. I'd give my right arm to get away from
this game.

ANDY: Ah, you'll be off the streets for good soon, girl. And
we'll be together—just the two of us. What could be nicer
than that ?

NELL: Sounds marvellous.

ANDY: It will be marvellous. Come on, let's have a go then.
Now watch. You need style first of all. And grace. Ele-
gance—deportment—

[*Tango music.*]

[*He shows* NELL *a few steps and invites her to try them out.
They dance. The sounds of the market are heard— people
selling, and people buying, heckling, quarrelling, laughing. The*

market erupts on to the stage. The main sellers appear and stand across the front of the stage—these include FRANK *and* NORA. FRANK, *his open suitcase suspended round his neck like a pedlar's tray, is festooned with his own goods—balloons, jewellery, windmills, monkeys on sticks, whirly birds, etc. etc.* CROSS-LANE NORA *too carries a selection of her goods on her person—silk ties draped round her neck, a few items of second-hand clothing in her hands. Everybody is selling.*]

NORA: Come along, ladies, high fashion at low prices. I'm giving them away. Silk ties half a crown a time—how about that, sir? Worth every penny of it—

JESSE: Here they are now, ladies and gentlemen, sixpence a time, as advertised on television. Last a lifetime. Sixpence each. And I'm robbing meself at that price. . . .

BARROW BOY: Apples a pound pears
Apples a pound pears
They're lovely
All fresh today
Buy while you may
Two pound a shilling.

TONY: Lovely violets, lady—sixpence a bunch—sixpence a bunch. Last a lifetime. Can't tell 'em from the real thing— lovely violets they are—fresh—perfumed too—

FRANK: Nothing on the tray above two and sixpence, ladies and gentlemen. And everything worth its weight in gold. . . . Something for the kiddies, sir? You want it, I've got it. . . .

NORA: A lovely pair of corsets, ladies. The very latest. We've never had a dissatisfied customer yet. . . . Four and six to you, madam. How are you doing, Frank?

FRANK: Not too bad.

[*They continue to sell. Gradually the other market people retreat from the stage.* FRANK *and* NORA *are left alone, selling each other's goods.*]

A — Cross-Lane Nora and Jesse push off Nora's
cart in a race, encouraged by Kit.

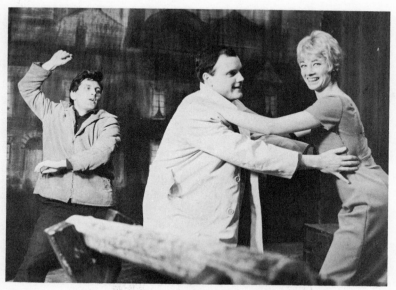

B — Banner dances with Nell; Andy keeps time.

C — Peg and Loll beneath the lamp post.

D — Frank and Kit, with Jesse remonstrating in
the background.

E — Andy and Nell try out a dance routine.

F — Nora and Frank talk over a cup of tea, while
Banner gets ready for a Saturday night date.

G — Peg and Jesse.

H — Frank and Kit.

NORA: Help the feller out, ladies and gentlemen. A balloon for the kid—penny each. That's not going to break you, is it? Monkey on a stick? Look at that. Hours of enjoyment.

FRANK: Silk ties—wear one of these and you'll feel a million dollars—

[*They are so engrossed in each other that they do not notice* KIT *approaching from behind. She watches them. She bursts the balloons with her lighted cigarette and goes off.*]

KIT: You dozey buggers.

FRANK: Well, we're not doing any good here, are we?

NORA: No, we may as well pack up and go home.

FRANK: Come on then.

[*They enter the house.*]

ANDY: Two weeks practice and we'll be a sensation, kiddo.

NELL: Sounds all right but what do we live on in the meantime?

ANDY: We're doing all right as we are, aren't we?

NELL: I thought I'd retired.

ANDY: You can't retire yet. We've got to live.

NELL: So we live off me.

ANDY: Just two more weeks. What harm in that. . . .

NELL: I might have known there was a catch in it somewhere. If there's any hard work to be done it's always the woman who has to do it. . . .

ANDY: I've got to work on the act, haven't I? I can't do two things at once, now can I?

NELL: Just two weeks—that's all. . . .

ANDY: There's a good girl. Don't you worry any more. Come on, I'll buy you a drink first, then we can go home and do some more practice there.

[*They go.*]

[BANNER *comes downstairs.*]

FRANK: Got a date?

BANNER: It's Saturday night.

FRANK: Busy boy this. Nice suit.

[NORA *feels the cloth with the air of an expert.*]

NORA: Good cloth. Nice bit of stuff.

BANNER: The best.

NORA: You're telling me.

BANNER: Hey, Dad, I think she fancies me.

NORA: You're a cheeky devil, you are. Just like your father.

BANNER: We can't help it, can we, Dad? If the women go for us. Had a good day?

FRANK: Not too bad.

BANNER: Let's hope you've made a profit.

FRANK: I'll get by.

BANNER: There's nothing like having a good solid bank balance behind you.

FRANK: If you can afford it.

BANNER: You should have married this one here. I bet she's worth a small fortune.

NORA: He knows he should have married me.

FRANK: When do you start working, son? You've been home for a good few weeks now—it's a good business you're in, whatever it is.

BANNER: Well, to tell the truth . . . I've chucked it.

FRANK: What?

BANNER: I've been thinking of . . . Well, I thought I'd like to emigrate, you know. I mean, well, it's supposed to be a good life out there. A couple of lads I was in the army with went out to Australia a year back, and they're doing all right.

NORA: And you're thinking of going over there as well?

BANNER: Yes.

FRANK: It's a long way.

BANNER: I might do well for myself out there—get a few quid together—I can always come home again.

FRANK: Aye! You can always come home.

BANNER: I've had a medical and everything. I should be able to go soon—next boat out there.

FRANK: It's all arranged, is it?

BANNER: More or less.

FRANK: Marvellous, isn't it? First time he comes home in two years and what does he tell us—he's buzzing off to the other side of the world.

BANNER: But. . . .

FRANK: No buts. You go, if that's what you want, and good luck to you.

BANNER: The world's a big place. I'd like to see more of it before they put me in a box.

FRANK: Don't start apologizing for yourself. You're going. That's all there is to it.

NORA: If you'd had any sense twenty years ago you'd have done the same.

FRANK: When I was his age I was a married man with two kids.

BANNER: And whose fault was that? Mine? Look, Dad. I'm young and single, not tied with a wife and kids. There's no reason why I shouldn't do and go where I like and when I like. And I'll tell you another thing—if I don't go now I never will.

FRANK: If you're not happy, go.

NORA: Take no notice of him, Banner, he's upset, that's all. He is your father, when all's said and done.

FRANK: It's all right. Forget I opened my mouth. It's a good thing to do for any young feller, I suppose. New country. . . .

BANNER: In a couple of years time you might all be able to come out there and live with me.

FRANK: Will you be going soon?

BANNER: Next boat.

FRANK: You've got everything together—money—papers and everything?

BANNER: Yes. You needn't worry about me. I can take care of myself.

FRANK: It's a good job you can. Nobody else is going to do it for you. You'd better get a move on or you'll be late for your date.

BANNER [*combing his hair and looking at himself in a mirror*]: God! I am attractive. I'm off then. Won't be late home, Dad. See you Nora. [*Exit.*]

FRANK: That's the life. Wish I was going on the town. Nice girl waiting for me, money in my pocket. It's a great life when you're young.

NORA: Don't kid yourself.

FRANK: He's a good lad, that, he'll always fall on his feet.

NORA: D'you think so?

FRANK: He doesn't seem to be doing too badly.

NORA: He doesn't seem to be doing anything. How much longer is this going on?

FRANK: What?

NORA: Don't say what as if you don't know what I'm talking about. You know what I mean. Kit and the rest of it. Do I hang about for the rest of my life waiting for you to do what you should have done years ago?

FRANK: Don't start that again. If she'd divorce me, all right.

NORA: Have you asked her?

FRANK: I don't have to ask her. I know her too well, and even if she did I've hardly got two ha'pennies for a penny.

NORA: I have.

FRANK: Oh! Aye! So you keep me.

NORA: I've kept better men than you in my time.

FRANK: Have you, indeed? It's the first I knew about it.

NORA: There's a lot you don't know.

FRANK: Would you have me under the present circumstances?

NORA: I'd have you under any circumstances.

FRANK: I'd never be able to marry you, Nora.

NORA: I'm not asking you to marry me.

FRANK: I'd sooner do it properly.

NORA: I know you would, but you can't do it properly, Frank.

and I'm not asking you to. But for God's sake, do something instead of messing about like this, I'm fed up with it.

FRANK: We're not a couple of kids having a fling, Nora.

NORA: We'll never have a fling at all if we keep on at this rate.

FRANK: It's too difficult, Nora.

NORA: Anything worth having's difficult. We can't keep on like this. You can't have your cake and eat it too, Frank. It's not good enough. It's not good enough for me anyhow, I've had just as much of this as I can stand.

FRANK: How do you think I feel?

NORA: I know how you feel but wouldn't you feel better if we were out in the open about everything instead of this hole and corner stuff. Kit wouldn't be any the worse off if you left her.

FRANK: I've left her before.

NORA: I know, and you've always come back too. But this is different. There's only one thing I want now and it's you.

FRANK [holding up his money bag]: That's all the money I've got in the world. I only ever have what I earn in a week. There's none in the bank and there's never likely to be.

NORA: Money's got nothing to do with this. Makes no difference at all who's got the money. D'you think I care?

FRANK: I care.

NORA: Then you care about all the wrong things, Frank. I've got money and you can always earn a living.

FRANK: You mean that, don't you?

NORA: Of course I do. What about it?

FRANK: It'd be a permanent thing, you know.

NORA: Anything'd be a damn sight more permanent than this set up. Don't worry about Kit. You've worried about her long enough. It's time to start thinking about yourself now.

FRANK: So what's the plans?

NORA: You make the plans. What do you want to do?

FRANK: Get as far away from this place as possible. A long way away.

NORA: That suits me. I'm ready to go tomorrow. What would you say to the pair of us setting up a little shop somewhere together, Frank?

FRANK: A shop?

NORA: There's a little grocer's shop up for sale out in Cheshire in a village there. Lovely little place too—we could turn it into a goldmine.

FRANK: Sounds nice.

NORA: It is nice, and it's not too expensive either.

FRANK: We'd be out in the country, wouldn't we?

NORA: That's what we both need. A bit of fresh air. We've been cooped up in this place too long. It's about time the pair of us had something permanent. This sort of life's all right when you're young but at our age you want something more settled. I've been on the market too long—longer than I ever intended—and this shop's just what I've been waiting for. Will you come out to Cheshire to look it over with me tomorrow?

FRANK: Sounds fine. It'll be a nice day out too—lovely place, Cheshire.

NORA: We could turn this shop into a good concern, Frank—not selling old clothes either.

FRANK: It's a smashing idea. We can get a surveyor in to look the place over to make sure it's all right.

NORA: And it won't take long to get the arrangements made for buying. We've got to move fast though—it's too good an opportunity to miss. You'll like the shop—it's a double-fronted place with tons of space and there's a little flat on top of it—not very big but it'll do for us—two rooms and a kitchen and bathroom. It only needs painting up and it'll look a treat.

FRANK: All that and fresh air too?

NORA: Yes. I've got the key—let's go and see it tomorrow, shall we?

FRANK: There's no furniture is there?

NORA: No—

FRANK: We'll have to get some then, won't we?

NORA: Let's get the shop first. Well then, that's settled once and for all. We'll go and look the place over, together—is that all right with you?

FRANK: Yes—it's fine.

NORA: And just remember, Frank, don't ever let money make any difference—money isn't worth it.

FRANK: Well, come on then, I'll treat you half a dollar's worth of cowboys and Indians.

[*Enter* LOLL. *They meet at the door.*]

FRANK: Evening.

LOLL: Hello, Mr. Fresko, is Peg ready for me yet?

NORA: She's still upstairs, fixing her garter.

LOLL: I'll go inside and help her with 'em then.

FRANK: Are you and the girl getting along all right together?

LOLL: Like a house on fire. Don't you worry about her—she's in very good hands.

FRANK: She'd better be. Well, don't bring her home too late tonight. Come on—

[FRANK *and* NORA *leave.*]

LOLL: Peg, I've arrived.

PEG: Hang on a minute, then.

[*He whistles while he waits for her to come downstairs.*]

LOLL: Ah! There she is, the girl herself. You're looking very smart. [*He starts to examine her suit very closely.*] This is a very nice piece of material, Peg, very nice indeed. Let's have a good look at it. Let's see how it's finished off—it's all in the finishing you know. It's a lovely job. Fits you like a glove.

PEG [*breaking away from him*]: Get away, you daft thing.

LOLL: What shall we do tonight then?

PEG: How much money have you got?

LOLL: Couple of bob—not much—Do you fancy going to the pictures?

PEG: Not again.

LOLL: How about a walk in the park.

PEG: Not again.

LOLL: Well, how about a walk around the houses?

PEG: Can't you think of anything new?

LOLL: Well, we'll stay at home then.

PEG: I've got all dressed up too.

LOLL: You must always get dressed up for me. I tell you what, let's get comfy. [*He sits on the sofa with his arms round her.*] Lean back. Ah! That's nice.

PEG: Is it?

LOLL: Yeah, suits me fine. I've been having some interesting talks with my teacher at school this week, Peg.

PEG: Have you?

LOLL: Yes. You know I finish my training in a couple of months.

PEG: Yes.

LOLL: Well, my teacher thinks he can get me a job with a big fashion house in London.

PEG: Can he?

LOLL: Sure. It's a great chance, Peg.

PEG: Are you going to go?

LOLL: Well, it's time I started looking towards my future isn't it?

PEG: Yes, I suppose it is.

LOLL: London's the place to be. Once I get stuck in there I'll be well away. The future's wide open. And I can make what I like of it. Don't you agree?

PEG: Oh yes, if that's what you want. What've you got there?

LOLL: Tickets.

PEG: What sort of tickets?

LOLL: Railway tickets.

PEG: You're all set to go, aren't you?

LOLL: A boy scout's always prepared.

PEG: I don't suppose they're return tickets?

LOLL: As a matter of fact, they are.

PEG: So you intend coming back?

LOLL: Oh yes! Always return to the scene of the crime. [*She snatches the tickets from his hand.*]

PEG: Day excursion to Blackpool. You fool! I thought they were tickets to London.

LOLL: I'll get those later. Are you coming with me?

PEG: What, to Blackpool?

LOLL: Well, both. Blackpool and London—when I go.

PEG: Come with you to London?

LOLL: Don't you want to?

PEG: If you ask me properly.

LOLL: Well, I'm asking. Will you come?

PEG: You've still not asked me properly. Are you thick or something?

LOLL: I don't know what you mean. It seems simple enough to me—I'm going to London; are you coming with me? Yes or no?

PEG: Come with you to London just like that?

LOLL: I thought that was the idea when two people love each other.

PEG: Has it ever dawned on you to ask me to marry you?

LOLL [*flinching as if the thought has only just struck him*]: Oh! Well. . . .

PEG: Oh! Well, yes?

LOLL: Being married doesn't mean anything—just a few oaths and a golden ring on your finger. I'll buy you a golden ring tomorrow if you want one.

PEG: It's Sunday tomorrow—the shops'll be shut.

LOLL: Does all that jazz really appeal to you—wedding rings and priests and choirs? Listen, Peg, if I went through it all the answer'd still be the same—I love you and I want to

live with you—we don't need any priests to tell us that. It's
simple.

PEG: And everybody'll be talking about us.

LOLL: Makes no difference—I'm the only one who should
matter to you.

PEG: You do, but I want to do it properly.

LOLL: Oh! You women, I'll never understand you. All right
then—I'll marry you if that's what you want.

PEG: Yes, well, thanks all the same but I don't think I'll bother.

LOLL: What d'you mean? You want me to marry you so I'm
asking you.

PEG: There are ways of asking.

LOLL: Well, marry me.

PEG: Oh! Go home.

LOLL: What's up with you? Are you going to marry me or
aren't you?

PEG: When you ask me in a proper fashion.

LOLL: But for heaven's sake I am asking you in a proper
fashion.

PEG: Don't just ask me to marry you for the sake of asking—
I'm not all that hard up.

LOLL: This is hopeless.

PEG: Don't shout at me.

LOLL: I'm going.

PEG: Get gone then.

LOLL: But I'll be back—and just remember—I want you to
marry me. [*They are both angry.*]

[KIT *enters.*]

KIT: Hallo—are you two still here?

LOLL: Hallo, Mrs. Fresko—it's a nice night, isn't it?

KIT: Yes—I think it's got something to do with the weather.
What are you kids doing staying indoors on a Saturday
night? You ought to be out having a good time.

LOLL: No money.

KIT: You don't need money to have a good time. I went out of this house this morning with five bob in my pocket but I've enjoyed myself on it.

PEG: Yes, well your idea of having a good time isn't ours.

KIT: If I had some spare cash I'd give it to you but I haven't—you'll have to get a job, Loll.

LOLL: That's an extreme measure, Missus.

KIT: Extreme circumstances call for extreme measures. Still, you mustn't take any notice of me—take no notice of anyone. That's one thing I've learned about life. Do what you like when you like it and as often as possible. When you get married, young man, to some sweet-natured wife, you still chase after the virgins and enjoy your life. And you must go to church every Sunday like a good boy and say all your prayers—then you can go home and beat up your wife and kick her downstairs. You know, love, I've been a bit of a devil in my time—I've consorted with criminals and I've cheated honest men but if I get the chance I'll do the same things again—because in this world it's the rogues and the villains who come off the best, so you look out for yourself and sod all the rest.

PEG: That's nice advice to give anyone.

KIT: Well, it's the truth. What is your trade, by the way?

LOLL: Well, I'm still studying at college—but I'm going to try and be a dress designer.

KIT: Oh—that's nice, isn't it? Here, have a cigarette.

LOLL: Thanks, Mrs. Fresko.

KIT [as PEG reaches for one]: You keep your hands off. You're too young to smoke.

PEG: Smoking's bad for you anyway.

KIT: Everybody else is out I suppose.

PEG: Can't you tell, it's so quiet.

KIT: Where's your dad gone?

PEG: Don't ask me, I'm not his keeper.

KIT: If ever a man needed a keeper that one does.

PEG: You're the one that needs a keeper.

KIT: Don't be so cheeky.

LOLL: It's my birthday today.

PEG: You never told me.

LOLL: I've only just remembered.

KIT: It's your birthday and you've had no celebration?

LOLL: None at all.

KIT: I'll take you both out tomorrow night. I'll treat you.

PEG: What with?

KIT: Oh! I'll pawn some of my jewellery.

PEG: How old are you?

LOLL: Never you mind.

KIT: It doesn't matter how old he is. He'll be just as attractive when he's sixty.

LOLL: Thank you, Madam.

KIT: It's true. You're a very pleasant looking young man.

PEG: Hey! Just you think on you're a married woman.

KIT: Just because I'm married doesn't mean to say I'm blind.

[PEG *goes to the door.*]

PEG: There's that stray cat over there.

KIT: Which one?

PEG: The marmalade cat who's having kittens.

KIT: Oh! Her. Poor little devil. She's half starved.

PEG: She shouldn't be. You spend more money on keeping her from going hungry than you do on me.

KIT: How much does a saucer of milk and a piece of meat cost? Don't be so selfish. Cats are always having kittens on that croft, Loll. Hundreds of 'em. But this marmalade cat's a wild one—won't come near you. She's like a little tiger.

PEG: Can we keep one of the kittens when they're born?

KIT: They won't stay put, love. We've tried before. What happened to the last one we had here? He was off and away —them animals are born wild and they won't settle down to living like we live. They've got more sense.

LOLL: I sometimes think it would be good to get back to the old days when we all went round in animal skins, running round with a chopper and clobbering any fair maid you fancied.

KIT: That'd just suit you, wouldn't it?

LOLL: It would, right down to the ground.

KIT: Back to nature.

[BANNER *jumps over the fencing round the tip heap. He is slightly drunk—just enough to make him aggressive.*]

BANNER: I'm back.

PEG: Oh! Here's Tarzan of the Apes.

KIT: Stop prancing around like a fairy elephant. And mind the furniture, it's not paid for yet.

LOLL: This your brother?

BANNER: Yes, it's her brother. And I suppose this little pipe cleaner in the jazz jacket's your boy friend?

LOLL: That's right, I am. Do you want to make anything of it?

BANNER: Oh! Hasn't he got a nasty temper?

PEG: Don't start an argument.

BANNER: He's a lovely looking little feller, I must say.

KIT: Now act your age, Banner.

BANNER: Look at the style of him. Look at that suit. Feel the cloth, see the cut of it. All dressed up for the Whit Week Walks just like the fairy on the Christmas tree. I just love your tie, darling.

LOLL: Well, of course, it's so me, isn't it?

BANNER: Everything about you is me, love.

LOLL: Ah! Shut up before I hit you with my handbag.

BANNER: Oh! He's shouting at me again.

KIT: Stop behaving like a couple of soft kids. You've got to make allowances for him, Loll, love. The trouble is he was conceived on a Friday night, after a fish supper.

PEG: Go and make a nuisance of yourself somewhere else.

BANNER: Shall I tell you something? I don't like your face.

LOLL: And shall I tell you something else? I don't much care for yours either.

PEG: Tell him to behave, Mother.

KIT: I can't tell him what to do.

PEG: You're hopeless, you are—

KIT: Go to bed, Banner, you don't look well.

LOLL: Shall I help him to bed for you?

BANNER: I'll put you to bed in a minute—permanently.

[PEG *drags* LOLL *from the house.*]

LOLL: Nice chap.

PEG: He has fits.

LOLL: I've met blokes like him before. They're all talk.

PEG: Forget him—he has fits.

LOLL: These big hefty blokes are all the same—all brawn and no brain.

PEG: Don't go on about it.

LOLL: Well, then. What is it going to be? I'm going to London. Are you coming with me or aren't you? Oh! I'll marry you if that's what you want—so long as you don't want a big posh do with white frocks and flowers and priests and choirs and all that jazz. . . .

PEG: That's only show.

LOLL: Okay then, it's settled.

PEG: No, it isn't settled really. You'd better think about it for a few days—you might want to change your mind.

LOLL: No, I won't.

PEG: Are you going now?

LOLL: Yeah, I suppose I'd better go.

PEG: I'll be seeing you then.

[*They kiss.*]

LOLL: Good night, Peg.

PEG: Good night.

[*Exit* LOLL. PEG *re-enters the house.*]

KIT: Well, cheer up—it may never happen.

BANNER: It will, you know.

KIT: This is a lively family, isn't it ? Look at her. She's standing there like a moonstruck calf. And I suppose you're
thinking again.

BANNER: I'm always thinking, Mam.

KIT: What about ?

BANNER: You'd have a shock if I told you.

KIT: You'd have a shock if I told you what I'm thinking sometimes.

BANNER: Don't be too sure.

KIT: Just look at that one there. Dead to the world and everything in it.

BANNER: That's love for you.

KIT: She's not in love with him, is she ?

BANNER: 'Course she is.

KIT: Well, you've let the family down, Peg. I thought you had
better taste.

PEG: You didn't choose a masterpiece.

KIT: That's no way to talk about your father.

PEG: Well, stop making fun of me.

KIT: She can't take a joke, can she ?

BANNER: No sense of humour. Girls are all alike when they
fall for a bloke, aren't they ? But fancy falling for a little
weed like that—

PEG: Stop insulting him—

[BANNER *creeps up on her and swings her round to face her
mother.*]

BANNER: Hey ! Look, Mum ! She's blushing.

PEG: Let me go ! That's all you're fit for—fighting old men
and young girls.

BANNER: Now you'll apologise for that—go on—down on your
hands and knees—kiss my boots and beg my pardon.

PEG [*breaking away from him and sparring with him*]: Oh !

KIT: Stop it! You'll be fighting like cat and dog before you know where you are.

[*He lets go of her. Silence.*]

PEG: Would you like a cup of tea, Mam?

KIT: I wouldn't say no.

PEG: Would you, Banner?

BANNER: Wouldn't mind.

PEG: Well—who's going to offer to make it?

KIT: Toss for it.

[BANNER *tosses a coin.*]

Heads you, tails me.

[BANNER *shows* PEG *the coin.*]

PEG: Just my luck. I bet that's a double-headed penny. [*She goes to the kitchen.*]

BANNER: She's got it bad.

KIT: Think so.

BANNER: It doesn't half make me feel old when I see her all dressed up to meet the lads. Still, she's a good-looking girl.

KIT: All the women in this family are good-looking.

BANNER: She'll be asking to get married soon.

KIT: D'you think it's as serious as that?

BANNER: Looks like it to me.

KIT: Oh well, I was younger than her when I got married.

BANNER: Why didn't you wait till you were a bit older?

KIT: Well, you know what it's like when you're young—you do everything in a rush—I did anyway. I couldn't wait—

BANNER: I'm going to wait.

KIT: You can't wait too long you know, sometimes, anyway—I didn't have much choice.

BANNER: How do you mean—much choice for what?

KIT: Getting married.

BANNER: Hey—it wasn't a rush job was it?

KIT: Yes, it was.

BANNER: I thought so. Just wait till I see my dad.

KIT: It wasn't funny.
BANNER: I think it is.

[PEG *comes back.*]

PEG: What's funny?
KIT: I am.
PEG: Has he only just realized that?
BANNER: She's got a sordid past.
PEG: She's got a sordid present. I don't know about anything else. Go on—tell me—all about it. What have I been missing?
KIT: You don't be so nosey. But just remember—when you're young temptation's great. . . .
PEG: And you couldn't resist it?
KIT: No I couldn't.
PEG: You ought to be ashamed of yourself.
KIT: I'm not ashamed of myself. I'm ashamed of other people.
BANNER: What time is it?
PEG: Time you were in bed if you ask me.
KIT: Are you still drunk?
BANNER: I'm not drunk. Never was. Can't afford it. Drink costs money and I haven't got any.
PEG: I thought you were coining a small fortune for yourself.
BANNER: Did you believe all that?
PEG: No.
BANNER: I had some money when I left the Army and I made a packet boxing, but I soon got rid of it. Everybody round here seems to think that I'm rolling in it, though.
PEG: That's the impression you give.
BANNER: I've always been good at making an impression, haven't I?
KIT: It's better to let people think you're on top of the world instead of going around crying poverty all the time. Anyway you'll be all right soon, son, when you're over in Australia. [*She steps outside the house.*] You might make your fortune there. Hey! Come here.

[BANNER *joins her.*]

Look—there's a new moon—don't look at the new moon through glass, Peggy, it's unlucky. And turn your money over in your pocket, Banner, then you'll always have plenty, like me, I don't think.

BANNER: Don't worry, Mam, we'll look after you in your old age.

KIT: Well, you'd better start now because that time's coming fast. Good night, kids. [*She goes upstairs.*]

PEG ⎫
BANNER⎭ : Good night, Mam.

PEG: How much longer are you going to be here?

BANNER: Till I go to Australia.

PEG: Must you go?

BANNER: Yes, I must.

PEG: Why?

BANNER: I just must, that's all. I don't know why. Might do well for myself out there.

PEG: It's such a long way. I'll probably never see you again.

BANNER: Well, you won't be missing much, will you?

PEG: Oh, stop martyring yourself. Anybody would think you're an outcast driven from pillar to post.

BANNER: I'll give you a clip round the ear if you're not careful. Have you no respect for your brother?

PEG: That's all you are—a great big bully. Well, I hope you're all right in Australia. I don't care what you do as long as you don't come to any harm doing it.

BANNER: You really do care what happens about me, don't you?

PEG: You're my brother.

BANNER: That doesn't make any difference to some people.

PEG: Well, I'm always the exception to the rule, aren't I?

BANNER: Always got to be different, haven't you?

PEG: Does no harm.

BANNER: Hey, why do you think my mam and dad carry on the way they do?

PEG: Don't ask me.

BANNER: Doesn't it drive you mad, living with 'em all this time?

PEG: I'm used to it, I suppose. Anyway, they're not as bad as all that. I've met worse.

BANNER: So have I, but that makes no difference. I don't care how other people behave. It's them two that worry me.

PEG: I suppose they're miserable. My grandad says it's only a phase but it's a phase that's been going on for as long as I can remember.

BANNER: Why do they fight with each other? Why don't they just sit down and talk things over?

PEG: Maybe it isn't as easy as that.

BANNER: It'd be better than all this carrying on. They seem to hate the sight of each other sometimes.

PEG: They don't really.

BANNER: Well, they put on a very good act then.

PEG: They still sleep together.

BANNER: How do you know?

PEG: Never mind how—I just know.

BANNER: Well, just because you sleep with someone it doesn't mean to say you love 'em.

PEG: I wouldn't sleep with anybody I didn't love.

BANNER: I should hope you wouldn't.

PEG: And neither would my mother—

BANNER: It's funny how you grow up, isn't it? A couple of years ago I thought you were simple-minded but you're all right now.

[JESSE *and* TWO OLD SOLDIERS *march on.*]

JESSE: Halt! Left turn. Now then, let's have a look at you. You're a sorry sight, aren't you? Look at him. What shall we do with him? First man to answer that gets court martialled. Let's have a look at your medals. That's a nice one—get it out of a cornflakes packet? What's that one for?

DERMOT: The last war, sir.

JESSE: And what did you do in the last war?

DERMOT: I tried to stop the bloody thing, that's all, sir.

JESSE: Did you now? Well, then, I want to see you all to-morrow down at the public bar of the Star and Garter. To rehearse for next year's reunion. No medals to be worn, boots polished and all spick and span. Company dismiss!

[*He watches them go off and turns to the house.*]

[*To himself.*] I'm a silly devil. [*He salutes* PEG.]

JESSE: Private Fuller. All present and correct, sir. Permission to enter.

PEG: It's your house, sir.

JESSE: Is it? I sometimes wonder. It's a good house, this. And if it could speak it'd tell many a good tale. They don't build houses like this these days.

PEG: No, I don't suppose they do.

JESSE: A fine old period piece. Good solid foundations. Not like these new council houses they're throwing up all over the place. Brick boxes with eyes in 'em! They won't last half as long as this one. . . . They won't. [*He enters the house.*] What's up with him?

PEG: Oh, he's a fraud.

JESSE: Never mind, son. We're all frauds one way or another. Don't worry about it, Banner. You fool 'em as long as you can because they're all fooling you. When I was courting your Grandmother I spun her some right fairy-tales. And I thought she believed 'em too. She didn't, though—not by a long chalk. Did neither of us any harm, though—got any cigarettes, Banner? Offer me one before I disgrace myself by asking for one. Thanks very much. Good smoke these.

PEG: You'll smoke yourself to death.

JESSE: Never done me any harm. I've been reared on brown ale and dripping bread—and I'm a damn sight healthier than three-quarters of the young men walking around today—[*Lights cigarette.*] I've enjoyed myself tonight.

PEG: How did it go?

JESSE: Everything passed off very pleasant.

[*He polishes the row of ex-service medals and ribbons on his chest with his sleeve.*]

There aren't many of us old soldiers left, you know. We're all going home fast.

BANNER: Well, this old soldier's off to bed. Did you know I am going abroad, Grandad?

JESSE: I had heard words to that effect. Australia, isn't it? I've been there. It was a rough place in them days. I expect it's changed now though. I expect it's been tamed like everything else. All people care about these days are washing machines, cars and television sets. They're so busy saving time but they don't know what to do with their bloody time when they've saved it. Civilization marches on—taking all the spirit out of life with it.

BANNER: Five weeks on a boat—and the sun too. Across the world it goes—via—Singapore, Aden, Gibraltar.

JESSE: Can't beat it, can you?

PEG: Sounds all right to me.

BANNER: Boat leaves Liverpool next week.

JESSE: As soon as that?

BANNER: No sense in hanging about.

JESSE: I'll have my own bed back then, won't I?

[*Pause, each lost in his own silence.*]

JESSE: Ta'ra then!

BANNER: Ta'ra, Grandad!

[*Exit* BANNER *upstairs.*]

PEG: I'll miss him, won't you?

JESSE: I will.

PEG: Still—it's his life. Your medals are sparkling. Polish 'em up yourself?

JESSE: Of course I did. Who else? Make a nice show, don't they?

PEG: Lovely.

JESSE: You know, love, these reunion dinners are losing their touch somehow—or else I'm getting too old for 'em. There were hardly any of my pals there tonight. Most of them are dead or waiting or too tired to bother any more. You remember my old soldiering mate, Harry Davenport?

PEG: The one with the whiskers?

JESSE: That's him, the old devil! He's gone. I went round to see him tonight and there he was—laid out in the front parlour dead as a doornail. He had a good innings though— he was getting on.

PEG: It's a shame. I liked him.

JESSE: Funeral's on Monday afternoon—half past four. Will you be coming?

PEG: I don't finish work till five o'clock.

JESSE: Never mind. They're cremating him. I'll ask them to keep him on a low light till you get there.

PEG: You shouldn't joke about things like that.

JESSE: I only laugh, love, for fear of crying.

PEG: Can I get you anything, Grandad?

JESSE: No. Harry got the V.C. in the First World War you know, Peg.

PEG: He's told me about it.

JESSE: The pair of us got honourable mention in despatches or something like that. God knows what heroic deeds we performed—as far as I can remember we were both blind drunk at the time. . . . Still, it's an honour.

PEG: Was that the Crimean War?

JESSE: Just how old do you think I am, girl?

PEG: Very old.

JESSE: Not as old as all that, I'll tell you. Though I've seen some changes in my time.

PEG: I'll bet you have.

JESSE: I've fought in wars but they were little 'uns beside the last one. Do you know something, child? It seems to me

we're not much better off than when we first begun it.
There seems as much trouble and strife as there ever was.
Still, that's the way of the world, I suppose. It's all the
same in the end. How's that boy friend of yours—Lollipop
or whatever they call him?

PEG: He's all right.

JESSE: You've got the same look in your eye as your grandmother had when she was courting me.

PEG: Have I?

JESSE: Oh yes, indeed! I was a bit of a deadleg in them days.
You know, footloose and inclined to be rather flirtatious
with the ladies. I'm still the same these days too.

PEG: If you were forty years younger I'd have you myself.

JESSE: I'd say you were rather keen on that boy. Am I right?

PEG: You're dead right.

JESSE: I thought as much. He's a lucky lad.

PEG: I'm glad you think so.

JESSE: You're a good 'un, Peg. A bit daft at times but none
the less a good 'un. You might not believe it but your
mother was just like you at your age. There's been a great
change in her though. Only to be expected, isn't it? Everything passes, they say, but it isn't so. Nothing passes—
everything stays with you. Everything makes its mark. You
mustn't judge your mother too harshly, girl.

PEG: She is a bit of a fool at times, Grandad. Oh, she's enough
to drive you mad.

JESSE: I know but you must try and understand, love, that it's
her age. Life's easy enough when you're old like me or
when you're young like you—it's when you reach the
chaos of middle age that the going gets rough.

PEG: I've never understood why my dad's stayed with her all
these years. . . . She's been nothing but trouble for him.

JESSE: He's stayed with her because he loves her, I suppose.

PEG: Not any more. He's running off with Cross-Lane Nora.

JESSE: He's been running off with Cross-Lane Nora for years.

PEG: This time it's serious.

JESSE: I'll believe it when I see it.

PEG: They're going to Cheshire to see about buying a business there.

JESSE: How do you know?

PEG: I heard them talking about it. What shall we do, Grandad?

JESSE: Keep well out of the way.

PEG: I think it's disgusting carrying on behind my mother's back. Someone ought to tell her.

JESSE: Don't worry, somebody will. I know how you feel, love, I feel the same way myself. It's a funny thing when people speak of me as an old man because I've discovered that the older a person gets the more he realises how ignorant he is and the less you know the younger you feel.

[*Outside, the* BEARDED PROPHET *returns home carrying his banner and whistling "Onward, Christian Soldiers".*]

PEG: What's that tune that man's whistling?

JESSE: I've no idea but it needs jazzing up a bit. Hey! Put a sock in it.

PROPHET: Good night!

JESSE: He's probably had a few beers. It affects you that way sometimes, doesn't it?

PEG: Yes.

JESSE: Well, I think it's time I was tucked up in bed. Hey! Come here, tell us a story, Peg. Go on. I'm fond of a good tale.

PEG: You're like a great baby. Tell us a story. . . .

JESSE: Does no harm. Come on, you've always been good at making up a good tale.

PEG: Well, all right. Are you sitting comfortably? Then I'll begin. It happened a long time ago. The weather was fine and there was plenty of food and good beer to drink. There was a country and like all good countries it had a King. He wasn't a bad old stick either, as Kings go, and his Queen

was a good-looking woman. So, he did his Kinging in the
daytime and his Queening in the night and everything
passed off very pleasant for everyone concerned. But like all
good things it had to come to an end, and soon the King
went off to war and the Queen was left on her own for
years. And naturally enough she got a bit fed up with it,
and one night when she was in bed she heard the West
Wind knocking on her bedroom door. Well, she knew what
he was after all right but she let him in all the same and
soon after he'd whispered a few sweet nothings in her ear
she succumbed to his passion and one thing led to another
and when she woke up next morning she found she was
pregnant. So—the West Wind carried her off to his palace
and when her husband came back from the wars and found
out that she'd buzzed off he was very upset. Anyway, after
a bit he got angry and he snatched a thunderbolt out of the
sky and threw it and he followed it to the place where it
had landed but his wife wasn't there. So he did the same
thing again and again until he arrived at the palace. [*Enter*
KIT *downstairs, in her dressing-gown.*] Well, by this time the
West Wind had got a bit fed up with the Queen and he'd
left her flat, her and her baby, and when the Queen realized
that her husband the King had caught up with her she felt
so ashamed of herself that she ran away with her child and
jumped off the edge of the world, straight into the sea.
And as soon as she touched the water she was changed into
a great rock.

KIT: Go on.
PEG: That's the end.
JESSE: Good story.
KIT: Make it up yourself?
PEG: Yes.
JESSE: Good story. It's time we were in bed.

Curtain.

Act Three

The time is a week later. Early Sunday morning. The scene is the same.

CROSS-LANE NORA, *pushing her barrow, enters.* JESSE *calls to her from the house.*

JESSE: Good morning, Nora.

NORA: Hello, love. Is it warm enough for you?

JESSE: It's cold.

NORA: There's just enough nip in the air to keep you on the move.

JESSE: Have a cup of tea?

NORA: I wouldn't mind.

JESSE: Hot, sweet and strong, like your men, hey?

NORA: I'd better sort this lot out.

[*She starts to throw out what she does not want on to the tip heap.*]

JESSE: There's a law against what you're doing, you know.

NORA: What?

JESSE: You're despoiling the face of our beautiful countryside.

NORA: Go on!

JESSE: Aye! There's a notice there. Look.

NORA: It could do with a coat of paint. Tipping prohibited. Five pound fine. By order of the Town Clerk.

JESSE: That notice has been there for years.

NORA: Well, I've never read it before. By order of the Town Clerk indeed. No please or thank you. There's too many people about these days telling everybody else what to do.

JESSE: Do as you're bid and be quick about it.

NORA: I'd like to put a bomb behind the Town Clerk. Banner hasn't gone yet, has he?

JESSE: He'll be off soon. Got a train to catch.

NORA: I shall miss that lad.

JESSE: So will I but what can you do about it? If the lad isn't happy here there's no use him stopping, is there?

NORA: He was upset last night, I think.

JESSE: You couldn't expect him to be otherwise.

NORA: No, it wasn't the best of send offs, was it.

JESSE: Farewell parties always bring out the worst in people. Everyone gets upset. The best thing to do is to sit in the corner and drink yourself under the table.

NORA: He's doing what he thinks best, I suppose. He's doing what he wants to do, anyway. You can spend too much time considering other people's feelings, Jess. You know that.

JESSE: I know it. Time for church.

NORA: Aren't you going?

JESSE: I'm waiting for Kit; we usually go together.

NORA: You're a right pair you two are.

JESSE: I only go to church because I'm fond of a good tune and it just so happens that some of the best music has been written for pontifical purposes.

NORA: What does Kit go for?

JESSE: Don't ask me.

NORA: I wish I knew. Whatever she goes for, nobody sees the effects of it.

JESSE: What's up with you?

NORA: You know damn well what's up with me.

JESSE: You're very fond of Frank, aren't you, Nora?

NORA: You know I am.

JESSE: I've been expecting you and Frank to float off any day.

NORA: We'd have gone weeks ago if I'd had my way.

JESSE: Well, what's stopping you?

NORA: It's not my fault we're still hanging about here. I had it all arranged to get a little business out in Cheshire, but Frank's been putting it off and putting it off and now we've lost the chance. He won't make up his mind.

JESSE: Well, it's a big thing. It isn't every day a man leaves his wife. Though I'll admit Frank does it more often than most.

NORA: If he loves me then it should be enough to make him break away.

JESSE: It should be, Nora.

NORA: Well, I don't understand what we're waiting for.

JESSE: There are other people to consider. What about the kids?

NORA: Does Kit care about the kids? She cares for nothing. By God, if I had two kids like that, they wouldn't know they were born.

JESSE: Well, we'll wait and see.

NORA: Time's flying, Jesse. We can't afford to wait much longer.

JESSE: Time is against you, love; if Frank were a young man it'd be different.

NORA: He's not too old to start again.

JESSE: I know, but there's too much holding him back. The time for Frank to clear off was years ago when he hadn't a wife and kids, but his whole life's here now, Nora, and he'll never get away from it.

NORA: I'll get him away from it.

JESSE: He'll always come back. . . .

NORA: Not if I can help it. I've made up my mind.

JESSE: Aye, but you can't make up Frank's.

[ENA *and* LENA *go past.*]

Good morning, ladies. Off to church. Aren't they a lovely pair? Hey, Lena, your stocking seam isn't straight. Come on, let me fix it for you.

LENA: Give over, you cheeky devil. Look at the barrow.

JESSE: I never see your husbands accompanying you to church.

NORA: The pub opens the same time as church.

LENA: My husband doesn't drink.

NORA: Only because you won't let him.

JESSE: You should never stop a man from doing what he wants to do. What he can't have by reason he'll get by force.

NORA: Imagine anyone taking her by force.

ENA: Are you throwing this stuff away? [*She pokes around the cart.*] I could use some of this.

NORA: It's rubbish.

ENA [*holding up a dress*]: This'd do for a put on!

LENA [*taking an old straw boater from the cart*]: Look at this, you remember when these were all the rage?

JESSE: I used to wear one and thought myself a smasher too. [*He puts the hat on.*] How's that? [*Singing.*] Sailing down the river—

NORA: You look like someone not right. Give it here.

[*She grabs the hat off his head and throws it to one side.*]

ENA: Don't throw it away, Nora, my kids are always dressing up. This is just the thing for them. They'll play for hours with it.

NORA: Just help yourselves, ladies. Take what you like. I don't suppose you'll pay for it.

LENA: You were only throwing it away.

NORA: And that's all it's worth too.

LENA: How's the family, Jesse? Banner getting ready to go, I suppose?

JESSE: Catches a boat tomorrow.

LENA: I bet you won't have Peggy with you much longer either, the way things are going.

JESSE: She doesn't miss a thing, does she?

NORA: No, she's all there with her lemon drops.

LENA: I've seen her about with that young Scotch lad. He's a bit of a fancy pants, isn't he? Does he work nights or something?

JESSE: What d'you mean?

LENA: Well, he never seems busy during the day. I just wondered what he worked at.

NORA: What business is it of yours?

LENA: Good God! I'm only asking.

NORA: Don't ask. Wait till you're told.

LENA: I believe you had a good party here last night.

JESSE: Yes, it was very lively.

LENA: We could hear it right down at our house. I believe the neighbours called the police in the end, didn't they?

JESSE: Well, somebody invited them but it certainly wasn't me.

LENA: I believe Kit broke out again, didn't she? Oh, she's a devil, isn't she?

JESSE: You can always rely on her for a good laugh.

ENA: It's a long time since I enjoyed myself so much as I did last night. I haven't laughed like that for ages.

NORA: You had a good time then?

ENA: Kit ought to go on the stage. She's a born comedian. A proper comic. She didn't half tell that policeman where to get off when he tried to take her in charge, didn't she? You know, Lena, she danced from top to bottom of this street with the bobby chasing her for all he was worth. Oh! You would've died laughing if you'd seen it.

LENA: Did they take her away?

ENA: Banner bailed her out, didn't he?

JESSE: Don't ask me. You seem to know more about it than I do.

LENA: The police ought to leave her alone. She does no harm, does she?

NORA: I bet you don't say that behind her back.

LENA: Hey, look who's over there. . . .

ENA: Oh, her.

LENA: She got married again last week, that one did.

JESSE: Is her first husband dead then?

ENA: Oh! No, she divorced him.

LENA: Should've been the other way round. She's been carrying on with that chap she's married to now for years. And they both had the cheek to get married in church too.

ENA: How did they manage that? I didn't think divorced people were allowed to get married in church.

LENA: That woman probably slept with the priest. Well, are you right?

ENA: No, I'm half left.

[*They go off to church.*]

JESSE: That's right, you two buzz along off and don't forget to light a candle for us both when you reach more hallowed surroundings.

[*The women go off.* BANNER *leaves the house.*]

JESSE: Are you off now?

BANNER: Yes, just about.

NORA: I've got something for you.

BANNER [*taking an envelope*]: I can't take this, Nora.

NORA: You're going to need every penny you can get hold of.

JESSE: Stick it back in your sky rocket, son, and remember this all your life—a woman giving a man money.

NORA: I can afford it. Have you had a good breakfast?

BANNER: Good enough. I can get some food on the train.

NORA: It's bad to travel on an empty stomach. You never know. We might be seeing each other again sooner than we think.

JESSE: There's not much I can give you, son, apart from my good wishes. But just think on this: honour all men, fear God and honour the Queen, and keep your nose clean.

BANNER [*stands to attention and salutes*]: Aye, aye, sir!

JESSE: You'll likely as not meet a nice girl out there, settle down and raise a little family for yourself.

BANNER: I might. On the other hand I might not.

JESSE: Can't beat family life, Banner. Women are funny things though. Look at my wife. A good woman, nobly planned. To warm, comfort and demand. She had a lovely figure, lovely hair and a skin like white silk—and she adored me. Get a girl like that and you'll be set for life. Mind you— a mother in law is a part of marriage that can't be escaped— like a wife—can't escape that either. I'll never forget the day I married your grandmother. She was married once before, you know—to a mate of mine, but he passed away while they were quite young and I nicked in and snapped her up. I went to his funeral and when we were coming back from the cemetery I shared the coach with the corpse's wife and I looked at her and I said, Mary you're the Belle of the Wake. Will you marry me? And by God, three months later she did. Said good-bye to your mother and dad?

BANNER: I've seen my dad but my mam was still asleep. I didn't want to wake her, you know.

[*Inside the house* FRANK *reads his newspaper.* KIT *comes down the stairs bearing the effects of the night before.*]

FRANK: Good morning, Kit? You're up early. It's only twelve o'clock.

KIT: Yes. I'm seeing how long I can keep up this Spartan-like existence.

FRANK: I'm glad you managed to get out of bed. I didn't think you'd ever get on your feet again after last night.

KIT: What happened last night?

FRANK: You made a public exhibition of yourself.

KIT: Did I?

FRANK: You did—well—

KIT: Well what? What am I supposed to say now? For God's sake shut up, Frank, and give me a two minutes' silence. I feel like death warmed up.

FRANK: You look like death too. . . .

KIT: Stop nagging me. Where's the kids?

FRANK: Your daughter's been up since seven o'clock and your son's just gone off to the other side of the world, more or less.

KIT: Twelve thousand two hundred and twenty-two nautical miles, to be exact.

FRANK: How do you know?

KIT: I looked it up in the library. So he's gone without saying good-bye to me, has he?

FRANK: He has.

KIT: It's just as well, I suppose. There would only have been weeping and wailing all round if I'd seen him and I'm no good at that sort of thing. Will he be all right, Frank?

FRANK: Of course he will. The lad can look after himself.

KIT: I hope so. Well then, that's that, isn't it?

[*She goes to the kitchen. Outside* BANNER *prepares to depart.*]

BANNER: Well, I'll love you and leave you.

NORA [*as he shakes hands with her and then with the old man*]: Ta'ra love, send us a postcard.

BANNER [*running off*]. I will, every port we stop at I'll put one in the post—ta'ra—[*He goes.*]

NORA: I wish I was going with him.

JESSE: I thought it was Frank you were after. Everybody seems to want to be going somewhere round here.

NORA: Frank and me might be going sooner than you think.

JESSE: Oh!

NORA: I've waited long enough. He's got to make his mind up one way or the other. And once we've settled it we'll be off. I've got to get right away from here.

JESSE: And Frank's happy with that, is he?

NORA: He'll be happy once he's made the break. I'll see to that.

JESSE: Ah well, we'll just have to wait and see, won't we? I'm too old and tired to worry about anything any more.

NORA: What's happened to that cup of tea you were going to make me?

JESSE: The pubs'll be open now. I'll buy you a proper drink. Come on.

[*They go off in one direction, then turn round.*]

Not that place, they've thrown me out of there. [*Exit.*]

[*Inside the house.* KIT *enters from the kitchen.*]

KIT: I don't suppose you'd come to church with me, would you?

FRANK: No, I wouldn't.

KIT: I didn't think you would. [*She takes stockings and blouse from the clothes-horse and during the following scene puts them on. She already has her skirt on under her dressing-gown.*]

FRANK: It always surprised me that that church doesn't fall down when you walk into it.

KIT: Aw . . . shut up. People like you make me sick. If you had your way there'd be a big notice outside every church saying 'SINNERS ARE NOT ALLOWED ON THESE PREMISES. KEEP AWAY.' Churches are for sinners. I'm the only genuine sinner there. All the other women sit there gawping at each other's hats.

FRANK: Churches are for repentant sinners.

KIT: I am repentant.

FRANK: Not for long. Look what happened last night. You were supposed to try and keep the peace for two years.

KIT: Let's face it, I'm not a very peaceful person.

FRANK: You don't need to tell me. What's going to happen to you in court tomorrow?

KIT: They'll fine me, I suppose.

FRANK: And what will you do if there's nobody there to pay the fine?

KIT: Then I expect they'll throw me into a prison cell.

FRANK: Don't you care what happens to yourself?

KIT: I care enough. I'll do myself no good by sitting down and weeping bloody great buckets of tears, will I? I'd sooner spit in everybody's eye.

FRANK: I don't know why I bother worrying about you.

KIT: I don't ask you to worry.

FRANK: I can't help it—

KIT: That's your bad luck then.

FRANK: As if I haven't got enough trouble to start with you have to give me some more. I've got enough on my plate to last me a lifetime. And you don't give a damn, do you?

KIT: So you say. . . .

FRANK: That boy's just gone to Australia and I'll bet it was you who drove him away . . . I bet we never see him again. . . .

KIT: Oh for God's sake, he's gone to Australia, not to Heaven.

FRANK: And before we know where we are Peggy'll be leaving home too.

KIT: Yes, I expect she'll be wanting to get married. . . .

FRANK: People'll always be in a hurry to get married, won't they? You'd think she'd have more sense, wouldn't you?

KIT: Aw, give over, it's not as bad as all that. Have you ever regretted marrying me?

FRANK: Every day of my life.

KIT: Oh well, I've never regretted marrying you, anyway.

FRANK: Haven't you?

KIT: What if I have? What good does regretting do? We've just got to make the best of a bad job, haven't we?

FRANK: That might be good enough for you but it's not good enough for me. This boy's had just about as much as he can take.

KIT: Has he?

FRANK: I'm not kidding. The day we got married, though it was a pretty poor bargain all round, I certainly got the worst part of it, didn't I?

KIT: Just because Nora thinks you're a little tin god don't start to believe it yourself, because it isn't true. . . .

FRANK: Don't bring Nora into everything. . . .

KIT: Oh, but I'm very interested in Nora. I want to know how much longer you're going to keep your little love affair on the boil, Frank.

FRANK: You'd have a shock if I walked out of here for good, wouldn't you?

KIT: Oh, don't tell me we're going to see a bit of action at long last. Don't tell me you've made your mind up to do something, Frank. Go on—get out of here, if you want to. I'm not stopping you. Go to your lady friend.

FRANK: I've had enough of this.

KIT: What about me! Do you think I enjoy it?

FRANK: You've had me for a mug long enough.

KIT: Then clear off out of it. Go on. A fine pair you'll make. You're both a bit old to start playing Romeo and Juliet . . . it's time you grew up, Frank.

FRANK: That's my trouble . . . I grew up too soon.

KIT: You've got a long way to go yet, but she's got the money, hasn't she, Frank? How long are you going to like living at her grace and favour? Well, go on. What are you standing there for?

FRANK: I won't come back.

KIT: We'll see. You've done this before—

FRANK: This is different.

KIT: It's always different.

FRANK: I'm going.

KIT: All right then. You've told me once. For God's sake get gone. And give Nora my best wishes.

FRANK: She doesn't need 'em.

KIT: No—she's used to dealing in second hand goods, isn't she? All I can say is this. I hope she has better luck than I did. I hope she doesn't wake up one morning and look at you lying in bed beside her and find love's young dream shattered at her bleeding feet. Go on—move. Or do you want me to throw you out?

[FRANK *leaves*.]

[PEG *comes downstairs*.]

KIT: Going out?

PEG: Yes.

KIT: You're never in.

PEG: I'm like you.

KIT: You could do worse. Where are you going?

PEG: Oh, just for a walk, I suppose.

KIT: With that lad?

PEG: Yes. Who else would I be going out with?

KIT: I thought you might be having a swop. A change is as good as a rest.

PEG: I don't want a rest.

KIT: You're looking very nice.

PEG: Thanks.

KIT: You and that boy make a good-looking pair.

PEG: Do we?

KIT: You take after me. Is he going to be around much longer?

PEG: Who?

KIT: Your boy friend.

PEG: Oh! Well, he might decide to move on. He's got plans and things but you know how it is—he can't talk about it yet. . . .

KIT: Has he got a job?

PEG: Yes.

KIT: In Manchester?

PEG: No, London.

KIT: Well, that's the way it is with men, they love you and leave you.

PEG: What would you say if I went with him?

KIT: It's your life. You ruin it your own way.

PEG: All right. Ta'ra.

[*She leaves the house and pauses as* KIT *exits upstairs, then she exits.*]

[NORA *returns for her cart.* FRANK *enters.*]

FRANK: Where have you been?

NORA: Eh?

FRANK: I've been looking all over the place for you. I went to your house.

NORA: Well, you can't expect me to be at your beck and call all the time, can you, Frank?

FRANK: No—

NORA: Well then—

FRANK: I got worried. I thought you might have eloped with the milkman.

NORA: You'd get a shock if I did something like that, wouldn't you? Anyway, I'm free to come and go as I please, aren't I?

FRANK: There's no need to start fighting about it. I've had enough fighting for one day.

NORA: Oh, have you been at it again with her? What was it about this time?

FRANK: You.

NORA: Oh.

FRANK: I've gone. I've left her.

NORA: How long for?

FRANK: I've left, left her, Nora. That's what you wanted me to do, isn't it?

NORA: Yes.

FRANK: Well, I've done it.

NORA: You won't regret it, love.

FRANK: I know I won't.

NORA: You'll be happy with me.

FRANK: Once we get away from here we'll be fine.

NORA: 'Course we will.

FRANK: But we've got to go now. No hanging about. We'll sell everything up. Get rid of everything. Sell your barrow— the lot—go somewhere different.

NORA: I'm not selling my barrow, Frank.

FRANK: Why not? You were going to sell it before. What about that business in Cheshire?

NORA: That's gone with the wind; I've got to keep my barrow, Frank. It's all we've got.

FRANK: Don't you want to get away?

NORA: Of course I do, but we can't jump out of the frying pan into the fire.

FRANK: You were going to sell your barrow. We agreed on that.

NORA: I'll sell it when we've got hold of something better.

FRANK: But there's no need to worry about things like that. Everything will be all right. I'll see to that. Trust me.

NORA: You're upset, love, come home.

FRANK: I want to get away. I thought that was what you wanted.

NORA: I do, but we can't just walk out of the place like that. First thing tomorrow we'll look for another business. We can't just rush off. Anyway, you have no clothes or things.

FRANK: All my things are in that house and I'm not going back there.

NORA: Then I'll go.

FRANK: No, you won't. She can keep everything. She can sell it. If I'm leaving then I'm leaving.

NORA: Well, there you are then, you must have clothes and things. You see, love, we'll have to make arrangements. Let's go home.

FRANK: I thought you wanted to come with me. What's wrong with the pair of us going now?

NORA: We can't, Frank. We'll go when we're ready.

FRANK: What am I going to do?

NORA: Just come and live with me.

FRANK: How am I going to earn a living? I'm not going back to that house for my suitcase. I'm finished with that lark.

NORA: You can live off me until we've sorted everything out. Then when we've decided what we want to do we'll do it.

FRANK: I know what I want to do. I want to get away from here.

NORA: I thought you wanted to live with me.

FRANK: I want that as well.

NORA: Have you come to me because you love me, or because you're fed up of Kit?

FRANK: I'm fed up with a lot of things. It doesn't matter why I've left her.

NORA: It matters to me.

FRANK: Let's go to the pub and talk this over.

NORA: No, love. I've had enough of talking. It is time for doing now.

FRANK: I want to talk it over.

NORA: Frank, if you want me then you must trust me. Come home with me.

FRANK: I'm going for a drink.

NORA: I'm going home.

[*They move off in opposite directions.* FRANK, *after a moment of indecision, follows* NORA *off.*]

[*A period of time passes.* KIT *enters down the stairs and sits. There is the sound of a railway engine being shunted back and forth along the line behind the houses. The street lamp goes on.* ANDY *and* JESSE *enter.*]

JESSE: Well, this is the parting of the ways then. I'll bid you a fond farewell—and good night. . . .

ANDY: It won't be a good night for me.

JESSE: What's happened then? Has your girl put you in the doghouse?

ANDY: Right in the doghouse.

JESSE: What have you been up to?

ANDY: Women are bloody funny things, aren't they, Jesse?

JESSE: I wouldn't deny that.

ANDY: You know me and Nell have been trying to work up a dancing act together—

JESSE: I've heard rumours—

ANDY: Nellie was always the one who kept nagging at me to get back into the business, so what happens as soon as I start? She finds out that I'm not as good as she thought I was. Now she's sulking. Won't speak to me. Won't even let me buy her a drink.

JESSE: That's the way women are.

ANDY: I never believed I was as good as she imagined I was. Anyway, even if we had tried to make a living in show business I don't think we would have been very successful. You can't believe in magic can you—not at my age.

JESSE: So you'll be staying here then?

ANDY: I didn't want to leave in the first place. I like it here. It isn't much but it's where I belong now, I suppose.

JESSE: It's good that you've discovered you belong somewhere. A lot of people never find out until it's too late.

ANDY: Yes, well, it's a bit late in the day for me to start trying to settle myself somewhere else. I'll leave all that new start stuff to Banner and the others. I'll make do with what I've got. If she'll speak to me.

JESSE: She'll start talking soon enough, don't you worry. Some women will have any sort of a man rather than no man at all.

ANDY: Thanks for the compliment. Good night—

JESSE: Mind the roads and don't talk to any strange women on your way home. . . .

[ANDY *exits.* JESSE *comes home.*]

JESSE: Anybody at home?

KIT: No, we're all out.

JESSE: Then I'll come in. Ah! It's good to take the weight off your feet. How's Kit?

KIT: She's all right.

JESSE: Been in all night?

KIT: Yes.

JESSE: Do you want anything?

KIT: No.

JESSE: Well, you can have that with jam on it.

KIT: You've no business being out on a cold night like this. Your health isn't up to it.

JESSE: If I did all the things people are always telling me I should do I'd be stuck upstairs in bed morning, noon, and night with a little bit of this for breakfast and a little bit of that for tea. You'd be feeding me on milk sops and jam butties. By God, you'd have me back in my cradle before I could turn round.

KIT: All right, then, you carry on and kill yourself if that's what you want.

JESSE: Kathleen, if it's got my name on it it'll find me no matter what I do or where I am—upstairs, downstairs or in my lady's chamber. Frank gone out, then?

KIT: Yes.

JESSE: Aye! I saw him down at the pub.

KIT: Then why'd you ask daft questions if you already know the answers? I suppose he was with Nora?

JESSE: Yes. They were having a very vigorous conversation.

KIT: I'm not surprised. They've got plenty to talk about.

JESSE: Don't worry, Kathleen, I'll see you all right. For all the money Frank brought home, I don't think we'll miss it very much.

KIT: We've done without it before.

JESSE: Aye, we have, and we haven't starved, have we? I can still do a good day's graft and I'm ready to do just that.

KIT: You're not thinking of going out to work at your age?

JESSE: A man can grow old, but old men aren't useless, Kathleen.

KIT: I never said you were. Don't worry, I'll go out and get a job tomorrow.

JESSE: You needn't bother; I've never lived off a woman yet and I'm not starting now. You'll be better off without him, love, all you ever did was fight.

KIT: That's life, isn't it. We've been fighting for twenty years.

JESSE: Enough to drive you mad.

KIT: Yes, but you don't go mad, do you. You just go on fighting and after a bit you get used to it and sooner or later you start to enjoy it.

JESSE: You'll get over it, Kathleen. A couple of months and you won't even miss him.

KIT: Well, what you can't have you just got to do without, haven't you.

JESSE: It'll be a damn sight more peaceful without him. For all the good he's done you, you ought to be glad he's gone.

[KIT *goes out of the house to the bombed site.* JESSE *stands in the doorway watching her.*]

KIT [*indicating the bombed site*]: The garden's looking very lovely this year, isn't it?

JESSE: A treat. Can't be everybody who has a genuine bomb site in their backyard. It's about time they shifted that load of rubbish. It's like living next door to a stinking slag heap.

KIT: You musn't be impatient, Dad. Can't rush these things. After all, it's only been here for the last twenty years. Is there any food on that table, Dad? Pass me a few odd scraps. Thanks. There are some cats over here—four kittens. Lovely little things. But they're very wild.

JESSE: Reared wild.

KIT: I was just thinking, Dad, about the night this lot got bombed. It's funny when you come to weigh it up. It's funny how you remember these things even when you think you've forgot, isn't it?

JESSE: Some things are forgotten too soon.

KIT: Chinese laundry used to be here, didn't it? And the toffee shop over there and there was a bank just up the hill, wasn't there? And it disappeared overnight. Remember it? When our Banner was evacuated to that school outside Manchester.

JESSE: Me and you went to see him every Sunday.

KIT: We did too and what a picnic it was. Every mother who had a son at that place used to trot out there come hail, rain or snow. It was funny really, when you remember the blitz and how we all met outside the church to decide how we could possibly get to the school without the bus. Then we all piled into anything on wheels—remember that bus with the flat tyres and all the windows blown out of it? We went on bikes and God knows what else. Talk about Muldoon's Picnic! We must've looked a daft lot. I'll never forget the faces of all them boys waiting for us at the school either. They all knew about the bombing and they were all wondering. Banner's face was a picture when he saw me roll up, but them boys whose mothers didn't arrive—I'll never forget their faces—Good God! I never thought there could be such cruelty in this Godforsaken earth.

[FRANK *appears as if by magic.*]

You're back.

FRANK: I'm back all right and if all the women in the world had one neck I'd break it with the greatest pleasure.

[*He enters the house and* JESSE *sings softly to himself.* KIT *calls to the kittens.*]

KIT [*simultaneous with Jesse's song*]: Come on, come on, puss. Chew, chew, chew . . . come on. I've got some food for you. Come on, don't be frightened of me. Food. There's not much of it, I must admit. A little bit of bread and a little bit of cheese. . . .

JESSE [*still singing*]:

> Winter's coming in my lass,
> The north wind's blowing cold
> I think we've courted long enough
> It's time our tale was told.

KIT: Ah! . . . it's a bugger of a life, by Jesus.

Curtain